PEOPLE POWER

AN ENTREPRENEUR'S GUIDE TO MANAGING HUMAN CAPITAL

SCHOLLEY BUBENIK

RENEE ALLEN PRESS
Lago Vista, Texas

PEOPLE POWER
AN ENTREPRENEUR'S GUIDE TO MANAGING HUMAN CAPITAL
BY SCHOLLEY BUBENIK

Published by
Renee Allen Press
Lago Vista, Texas

Copyeditor | Candy Zulkosky | TheWriterSuccessCoach.com
Cover Design and Interior Layout and Design | Yvonne Parks | PearCreative.ca
Index | Elena Gwynne | QuillandInkIndexing.com
Back Cover Copy | Lisa Canfield | CopyCoachLisa.com
Proofreader | Clarisa Marcee | AvenueCMedia.com

Library of Congress Control Number: 2018943329
ISBN: 978-1-7322822-0-9 (print)
ISBN: 978-1-7322822-1-6 (Kindle)
ISBN: 978-1-7322822-2-3 (ePUB)

SPECIAL THANKS

To my loving husband, Rick, who is always supportive of any new endeavor that I pursue. He inspires me and gives me confidence when I most need it.

To my daughter and business partner, Kristen Parrent, who provided me feedback and encouragement to write this book. She was extremely helpful when creating the recruiting and hiring chapters of this book.

To my daughter, Stacy Fanous, who has provided continued love and support throughout my career and understood at a young age the demands of entrepreneurship and a working mother.

To all the CEOs, business owners, and senior managers who provided different insights to their decision making processes and offered me the trust to be part of their senior advisory teams. I feel privileged to serve these amazing leaders who taught me much along my journey.

And lastly, to my father, Albert Buzan and mother, Peggy Buzan, for being great role models for leading with compassion and common sense.

TABLE OF CONTENTS

INTRODUCTION
The Young Entrepreneur   1

CHAPTER ONE
HR Strategies Are Important for All Businesses—Especially Yours!   9

CHAPTER TWO
Recruiting Strategies Overview   19

CHAPTER THREE
Compensation Strategies   31

CHAPTER FOUR
Recruiting Starts with the End in Mind   49

CHAPTER FIVE
The Hiring Process   65

CHAPTER SIX
Training and Development Strategies   81

CHAPTER SEVEN
Employee Retention and Engagement Strategies   95

CHAPTER EIGHT
Managing Risk Strategies   127

CONCLUSION   135

RESOURCES   139

INDEX   141

ABOUT THE AUTHOR   149

INTRODUCTION

THE YOUNG ENTREPRENEUR

I was twenty-four when I started my first business. I remember it vividly.

The year was 1984. I was at the University of Houston finishing my master's degree. Houston was flourishing from the oil boom. People were getting rich and I was ambitious and optimistic. It was soon thereafter that the oil bust hit Houston, but somehow, I grew my business in one year to the point of managing twenty-five employees, each of whom was older than myself.

I quickly realized I had much to learn about operating a business and about managing people. I knew I could not operate my business successfully without these employees. My hopes and dreams lay in their hands. It was a sobering realization.

My business was a private primary school. Student enrollment grew each month and I hired teachers and faculty at an expedient rate. I found myself in a predicament whenever one of them was absent or resigned because teaching isn't the type of job where positions can remain unfilled when someone is absent. I knew little about hiring, managing, or empowering employees. Amid my happiness for having a successful business, I felt overwhelmed and uncertain about how to manage the greatest asset of my company—my employees. I would come to learn what the term, *Human Capital* truly means. In those early days, I knew only that I could not hire fast enough.

• • •

1984 was way before the age of the internet. Any research I did, any information I obtained was found at the public library, in the basement of the local university library I attended, or from books I purchased in a bookstore. I also had my main confidant, my husband, who was one year wiser than I and served both as my sounding board and business consultant. We managed to fail at many things throughout the first years in business but kept getting better until we succeeded.

Seven years later, my school achieved national accreditation, many of my employees acquired early childhood teaching certifications, and my bottom line achieved profitability.

I attribute these accomplishments and my success during a depressed economy and with limited resources to the team and company culture I developed. I established relationships and a level of trust with my employees by being approachable and sincere. I shared information during troubled times and celebrated small successes with them when times were better. These actions are what I refer to as managing people with compassion and common sense.

One day I answered a random phone call from a business broker and things changed almost overnight. In response to his inquiry about selling my accredited school, I thought, "Why not?" I was 31 years of age and ready for a new challenge. In two weeks I sold my business, packed up my family, and headed back to my small hometown. I took a year off and taught half-days at the local elementary school. I had no specific plans for what I would do next. When I received a call from a school district administrator asking me to manage a program, which had just received a million-dollar grant, I eagerly accepted. I had experience managing an educational program, a budget, and employees. Over the next seven years my team and I developed the program, which became recognized as a model for similar programs throughout Texas. We achieved national recognition and I traveled to Washington, DC regularly to participate in a national study on family literacy.

How was I able to achieve this success in such a short time? I can tell you it was not by myself. I hired, developed, and engaged employees who shared my passion for the program and the families we touched. Together we shared a vision and purpose that drove us to accomplish what amazed many others. I remember being asked to present at the Texas Association of School Boards state conference. I was dumbfounded to be an invited speaker presenting to esteemed school district administrators and school board members, telling my story about how a small-town school district with few resources had managed to build this program to national acclaim.

MANAGE WITH COMPASSION AND COMMON SENSE

As I reflect upon the lessons learned during my early days as an entrepreneur and a manager, I realize how I manage human capital was—and is—my biggest success contributor. How did I acquire this skill?

The gift of being young and fearless allowed me to take risks and not worry about the failures I would encounter. Instead I set out to manage my employees like I managed my life, with compassion and common sense. I learned many of these skills from my parents and the environment in which I was raised.

My mother was an entrepreneur who owned a dress boutique in the small town of Taylor, Texas, just northeast of Austin. She demonstrated compassion and kindness the way she interacted with her customers. She taught me that success isn't always measured by instant profitability. It isn't just about the bottom line but about helping people. I recall young girls coming into her store needing a dress for a special occasion who could not pay in full. Or sometimes it was the mother whose husband was out of work and she could not purchase Christmas gifts for her daughter. My mom would grant them credit not knowing if she would ever be repaid in cash but knowing she would be rewarded in far better ways. Because of my mother's kindness, her employees saw first-hand how she cared for her customers. Through these endeavors, she gained the respect of her workers while obtaining customer loyalty. Not realizing it, she was truly setting an example of taking care of the customer with compassion.

My father worked at the local aluminum plant and was a community leader who served on the local school board, the sports boosters, and various community clubs. He was a natural leader who took on roles ranging from being captain of his high school football team to campaigning for a school bond needed to build a new high school. My father related to people who needed advice. Even as a young man, friends considered him a fatherly figure and knew he could be relied on to help in some way or another. He had a gift for empowering others to achieve what they would otherwise not be confident in doing. Many years after his death, I still hear from people who say, "If it were not for your dad, I would have never become an electrician or gone to college." Although neither my mother nor father obtained a college education, they learned and developed essential skills related to the people side of business and life. I recall many experiences from my youth watching both of my parents interact with people and manage conflict and situations successfully.

When I look at my own experience, whether in a leadership role as president of the school PTO, or as a business owner, or simply helping others develop their goals, I realize that I have inherited traits from both parents that contribute to my successes in managing human capital in my companies.

Managing People in Growing and Emerging Organizations

After several years developing and managing the educational program, I decided to expand my own education and get my PhD in education. While flipping through the *University of Texas Master's Degree Program Guide*, I stumbled across an executive program for Human Resource Leadership. Although I already had a master's degree in education, I thought it was time to make the jump to the corporate world and apply my management and leadership skills to companies. After twenty-four months, I finished the program and landed my first Human Resource Management position with a small manufacturing company.

I recall my interview with the owner. This was to be the company's first HR manager position. The owner's questions focused on employee-engagement. He wasn't interested in my HR credentials, nor my knowledge of HR compliance and administration. His focus was on employee well-being and strategies needed to achieve high level employee-engagement. I shared my ideas and was hired on the spot. We worked together for three years building programs and a company culture that remains in place today. In Chapter Seven, I will share these strategies and programs in more detail.

As the years passed, I moved from one organization to another, in multiple states, and managing up to 1,700 employees. I realized no matter how large or small the company, the challenges are similar. It also became clear that my destiny is to manage people in growing and emerging organizations.

Today, after thirty years of managing human capital and human resource departments for various companies, I run my own consulting business to help business owners develop and implement the human capital strategies needed to generate the success they envision. While I inherited my parents' ability to manage and relate to a diverse group of people, many entrepreneurs struggle in this area, as did I when starting my first business. It has become my purpose and my passion to help entrepreneurs and business owners navigate through the dilemmas related to the 'people side of the business', allowing them to avoid distraction and not get discouraged by the challenges they face. My tagline, *Your HR Business Advisor*, offers business owners and entrepreneurs more than a human resource administration solution, it offers an opportunity to serve as a key HR business advisor dedicated to their success.

Each business owner I work with is unique, yet each also seeks advice in common areas. It was this realization that spawned the idea to write this book so I could share my knowledge and techniques with a broader audience. Enough about me, let's move on to the purpose of this book and what you should expect to gain from reading it.

This book is designed for entrepreneurs, business owners, and managers who have found themselves with the dilemma of how to manage the people side of business. Each chapter addresses a fundamental HR function related to a key area of people management and provides strategies to consider and stories to illustrate them. This book is organized so that each chapter can be read and comprehended independent of the others.

The chapters include exercises for you to apply these concepts to your company and develop your own human capital strategies. Whether you are a business owner or just starting your career in management or human resources, the information in this book provides much more than the basics of HR and will engage you in a higher level of strategic planning.

What you will not find in this book is a HR compliance manual or the basics of human resource functions. We will address risk management as one of our strategies, but you can easily locate compliance information from your state or federal workforce entities. Also, the application of many of the employment laws and regulations are ever changing based on the most recent court ruling and litigation. Therefore, I strongly advise that if you have significant concerns regarding compliance in your organization, such as a prevalent issue or threat, you need to contact an employment attorney immediately. One phone call to an employment attorney may save you thousands of dollars spent combating a lawsuit. If you are wanting the basis of human resource administration, you can locate resources from the small business administration or other online resources that I will introduce you to in the chapter addressing risk management.

CHAPTER ONE

HR STRATEGIES ARE IMPORTANT FOR ALL BUSINESSES —ESPECIALLY YOURS!

I think all entrepreneurs and business owners would agree that your employees are one—if not the most important—asset of your company. Are you aware, as I am, of how important the way in which you manage your *people processes* can greatly affect your bottom line? When I first began my career in Human Resources I explained my profession to others as the Personnel Department because that term was among the first associated with my profession. I didn't like this term because I did not want to be considered as the administrator of employee paperwork. I wanted to be the Chief People Officer, the CPO who developed ways to improve human resource functions that directly impacted the bottom line and contributed to the overall success of the company.

I soon discovered many HR professionals were simply administrators. I recall during my training for a large company that I sat with each HR specialist to learn about their duties and how they were performed. I asked the same question to each person, "Why do you do it this way?"

I got similar responses from everyone, "Well, that is the way they told me to do it." "That is the way we have always done it."

I quickly realized they were simple HR administrators completing paperwork. They did not appear to be engaged in the bigger picture. They only saw the meaning or purpose of their work as it related to themselves. Each completed assigned tasks unaware of possible contributions to improving processes or of the positive or negative impact their duties have on their department or the organization.

As a strategically wired person, I saw the potential in this situation and knew I would take on a much bigger role than being simply the Personnel Department. I would take what I learned from this experience and improve the processes to achieve better results. I aspired to engage with the other executives and help them succeed by managing their human capital. I was once a business owner and I knew first-hand the challenge and distraction your employees could create for your operation. This is an advantage I had over many of my peers in the Human Resource profession and most likely the reason I performed as a strategic business partner instead of an administrator.

I have realized throughout the years not everyone likes the HR Department. Perhaps it is because many HR professionals are rigid and rule-based instead of strategic and solutions oriented.

Some tend to have no sense of urgency, are slow getting things completed and struggle to keep up with the pace of an emerging business. Therefore, I don't know that all business owners view Human Resources as an integral part of their business strategy. If you have that mind set, I'm hoping to change your mind in this book.

> **What most people don't understand is that managing people processes is more than administering state and federal regulations and managing the paperwork.**

Your people management should be a well-developed plan much like your business plan or your marketing plan. Your human resource functions should be developed to align with your company's business goals and culture. It is much more than administrating standard operating procedures. Your human capital strategies should serve as a link between your HR management and the overall strategic plan of your company. These strategies encompass a variety of areas carefully directed at achieving your business goals and giving you a competitive edge.

WHAT DOES THIS LOOK LIKE?

Sounds simple? You need answer only two questions to effectively develop human capital strategies:

1. **What kind of people do I need to manage and run my business in a way that aligns with my business goals?**

In your answer, consider that each company is unique, as are the people running the company. Think about key management and work your way through your organization. You need to identify and understand the personality traits, skills, abilities, values, and perceptions that your management team needs to embody and encourage in order to align with your business strategy. Then you will need to conduct a more thorough workforce analysis to identify the same for the other positions within your company. We will go into more detail for developing your workforce plan in Chapter Four.

2. **What programs and initiatives should I implement that will attract top talent, achieve employee retention, and develop my employees?**

Although there are many areas of human capital strategic planning, our focus is on areas that impact emerging companies the most. There are five strategies critical to successful execution of your overall strategic HR plan. If you miss one, the other strategies will suffer. These strategies impact who you hire and the way your employees feel about your company. They define the employee benefits and programs you provide that attract, educate, develop, and empower your workers. The results are intended to increase employee satisfaction, performance, and retention. In addition, these programs enhance the employee's experience, interaction, and communication with management.

So why are these strategies so important to your company? Employee performance and attitude affect every part of your business. Happy employees have a higher commitment to their job, go above and beyond the call of duty, and have better attendance. They carry these attitudes through their interactions with your customers and interact more positively.

Employee behaviors affect your financial outcomes as well. Loyal employees seek ways to work efficiently, cut costs, and provide valuable feedback for improved results. On the contrary, high turnover rates are linked with increased HR cost associated to recruiting and new hire training that negatively impact your bottom line.

Lastly, disgruntled employees retaliate against their employers resulting in discrimination claims and lawsuits, not to mention bad press.

I hope I have convinced you that your HR strategies are good for employees and good for your bottom line. To remain competitive in today's market, companies need to develop and implement strategic initiatives that capture behaviors and trends in the industry. Being proactive rather than reactive will determine your competitive advantage regardless of your company size.

Now, let's review *The Five Strategies* for managing the people side of your business that will be discussed in this book and questions to stimulate your thoughts.

#1 Recruitment Strategies

Hire the best talent; those with the experience and credentials, and those who truly align with your company culture and fit in with the group. What does top talent look like? This includes more than SKAs (skills, knowledge, and abilities). It includes the behaviors and traits one needs to work collaboratively in your company, with other team members, and with your customers. Where will you find this talent? How will you portray your company so top talent will be attracted to work for you? What does your company offer to entice people to work for you? These questions and your answers lead into the next strategy.

#2 Compensation Strategies

What is your compensation philosophy and what will your compensation package include? Determine where in the general market your company wants to position itself with regards to salary—mid salary range, lower twenty five percentile, or top twenty five percentile. Most companies think of compensation only in terms of salary and bonuses. Total compensation includes health benefits, time off work, and holidays as well as special perks like working from home, time off to volunteer at local nonprofits, rewards and recognitions, casual dress code, and the breakroom goodies. Also consider how you can use your benefits to offset areas where you are not highly competitive.

#3 Training and Development Strategies

Some companies are unable to offer highly competitive salaries and benefit packages. One way to offset this problem is to develop a training program with clearly defined career-development paths for your employees. Job seekers today are looking at more than salary when deciding on employment. A company that offers a training program and develops their people can be more attractive than salary alone. Creating and implementing effective training programs are attractive to both employees and management because they offer a way to develop your employees, which contributes to employee retention thus increasing productivity and profitability.

#4 Retaining Top Talent Strategies

In addition to training and development programs that contribute to retaining top talent, ensure that your management team develops a culture of respect in the workplace and instills your important company core values. Are your managers effective in motivating and engaging your employees? Do you establish and communicate clear expectations to your employees and provide regular feedback and dialog? Do your employees believe your company is a good place to work? Do your company values align with your workforce?

#5 Managing Risks

Managing risk is the most feared among management when thinking about human resources. Avoiding lawsuits and knowing how to navigate through troubling times, compliance, overtime regulations, and the ever-changing employment laws are concerns of most organizations. I have found if you implement the right strategies for the other four areas, then managing risk is minimized.

Now it's your time to develop your strategies. Below is the first exercise to complete for your HR strategic-planning process. I encourage you to invite others, such as your key business partners or management team, to help you complete this exercise.

EXERCISE
Human Capital Strategic Questionnaire

Assess your company's current strategy to gain a deeper understanding of the areas that you need to address. Keep in mind that every company is different due to their size, infrastructure, and industry. I have also found that a company's development phase—whether it is in start-up, expansion, or status quo—also requires different approaches to their human capital strategies.

Recruiting	
Do you have a clearly defined recruitment strategy that is successful in finding and hiring the top talent you need for your organizations?	

Have you created a workforce plan that includes the positions necessary for your company's growth and attrition? The list should include the skills and traits needed for success in each position. Have you created a timeline for vacancies due to turnover and new positions required for growth, so you know when to begin recruiting for these positions?	
Are your hiring managers trained and confident in their hiring processes?	
Is your hiring process efficient in both time-to-fill and cost effective?	
Compensation	
Do you have a written compensation philosophy?	
Does it address strategies related to the total compensation including benefits such as medical, retirement, personal time off, and special perks?	
Do you evaluate the current market regarding salary levels in your industry?	
What benefits do you offer your employees related to medical, dental, and retirement?	
Are you satisfied with your benefit offerings?	

Training and Development	
Do you provide onboarding and new-hire training to ensure job success for new employees?	
What training programs does your company offer or promote?	
How do these programs support a career-development path?	
Retaining Top Talent	
Are you successful hiring top talent and is it a priority?	
What is your turnover rate for employee retention?	
What is the real reason for employees leaving?	
How would your employees describe your company culture?	
Is your management team successful at motivating and engaging employees?	
Managing Risk	
What areas or concerns do you have regarding risks related to your employees?	
What employment regulations apply to your company?	
When is the last time you conducted a human resource audit regarding classification of exempt employees, independent contractors, employee personnel files, and I-9 processing and documentation?	

CHAPTER TWO
RECRUITING STRATEGIES OVERVIEW

RECRUITING IMPACTS YOUR BOTTOM LINE

You may have a great business plan, a great product or a great service, but do you have the right people to execute your plans and drive you to profitability? Many entrepreneurs and managers rarely take the time to analyze this quandary. We are so consumed with operations, sales, and the bottom line that we often overlook or neglect planning and implementing recruiting strategies. I once worked with an established company of fifteen years and they rarely recruited anyone—meaning they did not advertise job vacancies nor did they develop any recruitment process. Instead, they depended on their employees and business acquaintances to send them referrals. They would meet with candidates and if they liked them, they would hire them. As you can imagine, this did not always work out well.

> Do you have the right people to execute your plans and drive you to profitability?

Why is developing a recruiting strategy important in the hiring process? Let's look at a few statistics related to recruiting and hiring.

- The U.S. Department of Labor estimates that the average cost of a bad hiring decision can equal 30% of the first year's earning
- The average settlement of negligent hiring lawsuit is nearly $1 million
- Studies show that as much as 80% of employee turnover is due to bad hiring decisions

I hope I have grabbed your attention. In addition to the financial burden that comes with hiring the wrong person, companies experience a range of negative outcomes. Typically, companies see a decline in employee morale because employees become disheartened when they see their co-workers leaving. Your company's reputation can be damaged from disgruntled, departing employees who post derogatory comments on social media outlets. Even worse, your business can suffer from poor customer service or productivity affected by employing people who simply cannot perform their job duties.

ARE YOU HIRING THE RIGHT WAY?

Recruiting is vitally important to your company. Companies that excel in recruiting generate 3.5 times more revenue growth than their inferior peers. Studies show recruiting is the most important human resource function when it comes to the return on investment.

> **Companies that excel in recruiting generate 3.5 times more revenue growth than their inferior peers.**

When you do not hire the right talent for your company, all human resource functions are adversely impacted. Employee relations, employee turnover, company culture, team cohesiveness, and employee productivity are a few that come to mind.

Most of us have experienced the effects of a bad hire. Hiring the right people is a process. I have developed strategies for successful hiring that I refer to as the Right Source Method. This method ensures that your recruitment efforts result in the best hires possible. The Right Source Method is described in Chapters Four and Five.

THE WAR FOR TALENT

It doesn't require too much convincing for you to agree that your goal to hire and retain top talent is a smart business decision, but did you know many studies indicate there is a war for talent in our current economy? This means that as the U.S. economy continues to grow, the demand for talent exceeds the supply of bright, talented individuals. Companies are finding the search for top talent is costlier, lengthier, and more difficult. Hiring practices must be adapted. The time it takes to fill a position is critical. Employers must make hiring decisions quickly to avoid losing qualified candidates to other companies. In the new economy, retaining top talent (which we will address in Chapter Seven) becomes instrumental because people are willing to change jobs more frequently, and social media makes it easier to find and approach people with new job opportunities. Passive job seekers (those not actively looking for a new job but willing to jump ship if the right opportunity presents itself) are the target for many recruiters to hire their competition's talent.

WHAT THIS MEANS IN TODAY'S COMPETITIVE MARKET

Companies can no longer be complacent and reactive. They cannot believe they are immune to this economy and environment. Now, companies must realize it is as important to be as focused in defining recruitment strategies as it is marketing strategies. Begin with developing key strategies to combat these circumstances.

> Developing a set of recruiting strategies will better position your company to compete in today's market.

Ensure your hiring managers are properly trained in both legal hiring and recruitment best practices. The remainder of this chapter will provide exercises to stimulate your thoughts and develop your processes.

EXERCISE
Begin by assessing your company culture.

Which of the following best describes your company? (You can choose more than one.)

- A large company with more resources and opportunities for employees to develop and grow
- A small company that is growing and a great place for

employees to position themselves and make a mark

- A recognized company that is a leader in the market and open for new hires to join the team of winners
- A successful and established company that provides financial stability and longevity for employment (as compared to a start-up)
- A fast-growing company with an entrepreneur spirit looking for entrepreneurial-spirited individuals in a creative, non-bureaucratic environment
- A start-up company where you can wear many hats and learn new skills
- A philanthropic or humanitarian organization dedicated to a worthwhile mission that is open for new hires who are caring individuals not focused on self-indulgence
- A lifestyle company interested in work-life balance that believes happy employees nurture profitability

The next step of the process is to identify what makes working for your company special. This is considered branding. You may already have branding with your marketing strategies for products or services. Apply the same strategy here. Consider how you will communicate your value-added proposition to future employees as well as existing employees.

EXERCISE
Developing Your Recruiting Pitch

You may already have ideas and an understanding of what makes working for your company special. I strongly advise collecting information from your employees as well. This is important because you may have false assumptions or miss critical information. One way to do this is to conduct individual meetings with your key employees and managers. Ask what they like about working at your company and why they decided to join your team. Ask them to describe the perks of working for your company.

List employee comments about what they like about working for your company.

_____

_____

_____

What are they saying about the special perks that your company offers?

_____

_____

_____

Why did they decide to work for your company?

_____

_____

_____

List your additional comments in area below:

_____

_____

_____

Next, list the benefits of working at your company. Be sure to include all your offerings (compensation, time off, company culture, health benefits, retirement benefits, training and development).

_____

_____

_____

Next you will develop your company recruiting pitch to tell a meaningful story about your company. Include the information you have collected that emphasizes your value-added proposition to prospective employees. Involve your marketing team and key employees to help you further expand your story to include your history, leaders, mission, community involvement, and any company awards or recognitions. Your sales people may be especially talented in developing one as well.

I have provided a recruiting pitch sample for you to review below:

I would like to share some background information about our company. We are a well-established manufacturing company that has been in business about twenty years. Our company's founder and CEO created the company on the principles of the book "Built to Last" and has accomplished just that. Throughout the ebbs and flows of the technology industry, he has managed to establish a financially strong foundation and grow the business over the years. He and the management team built a company culture that embraces entrepreneurship and believes in developing their people. Our company has established training programs and provides opportunities for employees to advance. In fact, many of our employees worked for the company many years and advanced to management and leadership positions.

The company believes in structuring compensation to include excellent benefits, especially for a company their size in this industry. They contribute 100% to medical benefits and offer dental, vision, and a 401K program. This year we added a sick bank that allows employees to donate their PTO hours to be used by co-workers who encounter serious medical and family issues.

In addition to investing in their people, the company invests in the community. You can view the many volunteer and community programs they sponsor on our website. We refer to our work here as purposeful employment where people work and receive more than a paycheck.

A GAME PLAN FOR WINNING THE WAR ON TALENT

What can you do to help address the supply and demand problem for recruiting? In addition to creating an awesome recruiting pitch, there are other strategies that will increase your ability to attract more job candidates. Here are examples of strategies that can help you in this area:

Implement an employee referral program where employees receive a small bonus or gift for referring candidates that are hired. This is easily accomplished by printing standard business cards that contain your company information and website and instructions on how to apply. Ask employees to distribute the cards to others who they think would be great prospective candidates.

Send weekly emails to your employees with job postings for open positions. Encourage them to post these on their social media accounts and to forward them to friends and associates they recommend for employment at your company.

Use your social media accounts. Post job openings on your news feed or provide a link to your company job page. Another use of social media is to engage with prospective employees by connecting with them. Your company may want to post jobs on various group pages or websites related to your industry. Work with your marketing department to ensure that your company's social media sites contain information related to the attractiveness of working for your company.

If you are needing to hire multiple positions or opening a new location, **host a career fair** at your location or at a meeting place in your community. Create an event on social media sites and send electronic invitations to the community at large. Include business owners and business associates, prospective employees, educational leaders, industry leaders, and local state employment agencies. Work with your marketing department to provide the marketing initiatives to attract people to your event.

Begin building a pipeline of job candidates. Sometimes you may have multiple qualified candidates but can only hire one, so stay engaged with prospective employees. Again, work with your marketing department to develop a social media marketing campaign to engage with future employees. Then you can build a pipeline in an applicant tracker system of the prospects as you engage with them. However, if your company doesn't have a need for this system, you can always store information in a prospect file or create a prospect list.

Always treat your prospective employees as customers. This was one of my first goals after being hired at one company where my experience as a prospective employee was horrific. Here is a recap of my experience:

Upon arriving for the interview, I was acknowledged by an unfriendly person who instructed me to, "Sit here and wait until we call you." I was then herded into a room with other candidates and issued a test. I was asked to wait until my name was called. There were no smiles or warm welcoming, even when I was called to the room to interview. I remember questioning whether I wanted to pursue this opportunity at all. It wasn't until the second round of interviewing with my soon-to-be-manager, that things warmed up.

I was offered the job and accepted but decided the first thing I was going to change was the recruiting process. I trained my recruiters and hiring managers to treat every job candidate as if they were a customer. Not only is your company's reputation at stake, but it is the right thing to do. Over years of interviewing thousands of candidates, my recruiting team continues to receive compliments and thank you notes for being courteous and respectful.

Add a career page to your website and include information that communicates the benefits of working for you, training programs, community-involvement activities, and employee well-being programs. Include testimonials from employees, either text or video. Make sure you keep job postings updated and have a place for candidates to submit their resume. Even small companies can create an email address for incoming resumes at no cost. For example: gethired@yourcompany.com.

Implement a career-development program and advertise it as part of your benefit package. I once worked for a company that had a difficult time attracting candidates due to their low salaries and remote location. To attract and retain top talent, we created a career-development program and began marketing this to prospective candidates during our phone screening process. The program provided training that rewarded employees with pay raises as they completed each phase. The program was a huge success, allowing us to attract, promote, and retain top talent. Candidates were willing to work for us at a lower wage knowing they would be trained and promoted to a higher paying position based on their performance.

Implement an onboarding training program for new hires. The war for talent includes recruiting and hiring strategies, and retaining the newly hired team members. Both are essential to winning this war. Below are some statistics about onboarding employees:

- 69% of employees are more likely to stay with a company for three years if they experienced great onboarding
- Up to 20% of employee turnover happens in the first 45 days
- Nearly 33% of new hires look for a new job within their first six months on the job

You can see that once you hire the employee, retention is the next key strategy for the war on talent. Additional information will be provided in Chapter Seven when we cover onboarding training.

Establish a well-documented standard operating procedure for recruiting. Be prepared to replace an employee before terminating him/her. This may sound unjust but it can be necessary to maintaining uninterrupted business operations.

EXERCISE
Identify strategies for Your Game Plan
for Winning the War on Talent

Now take a moment to consider these strategies and determine which strategies fit your company culture and can increase your pool of candidates. Meet with your marketing and management team to brainstorm the possibilities and record them below:

_____

_____

_____

_____

_____

_____

_____

_____

_____

CONCLUSION

Recruiting top talent is one of the most important strategies in the human capital arena. Developing strategies for identifying and marketing to prospective employees is critical for winning the war on talent. Many strategies have been presented in this chapter that are simple and affordable and can yield high results. Incorporate these strategies in a recruiting plan. Train your team how to develop and execute your recruiting plan and you will improve your hiring results.

CHAPTER THREE

COMPENSATION STRATEGIES

It is important to develop your compensation strategies before you set out to recruit employees.

A strategic plan for employee compensation determines how much you will pay for each position and the employee benefits you will provide. It should be developed with several things in mind including what type of employee you want to attract and how you are going to retain these employees once hired. If you do not establish a compensation strategy, you may be faced with issues related to pay equity within your company as well as problems with recruiting top talent. A successful compensation strategy will equip your company to compete in the market for the best employees.

Attracting quality employees is a primary reason for developing compensation strategy because no matter how well you recruit, if your compensation package is not attractive and competitive, you will fail in this area. Either you will not be able to attract them to accept your offer of employment or they will leave for a more lucrative compensation package later.

Compensation pay is not always apples for apples, meaning that compensation packages will vary according to industry, geographical location, and company size. For example, an accountant working for a large financial institution may be paid differently from an accountant working for a small manufacturing company. Although you may not be able to compete with the larger companies, your recruiting strategies should take this into account. You may elect to target job seekers from companies similar to your size and industry.

Another major reason for developing compensation strategies is to encourage employee retention. Establishing a compensation program that rewards employees for their seniority in the company can promote loyalty and longevity; however, other rewards should also be included that are tied to employee performance and results. Developing a rewards system such as a bonus plan tied to individual employee performance or to company performance will add value to your compensation program and increase employee productivity and profitability.

Strategies for retaining employees is more than mere compensation. They include effective onboarding, relationships and interactions with management, company culture, training, and career opportunities. We will address these strategies in Chapter Seven, Employee Retention and Engagement.

PLANNING AND DESIGNING
YOUR COMPENSATION STRATEGY

The first step in this process is to decide how your pay rates are going to compare to the rates of pay in the market. You will have several options to consider in determining your pay philosophy. The first is whether you want to match the market. This is one of the most common strategies because it will ensure that you remain competitive in today's job market. If you adopt this option, you will need to review the market every year or so to ensure that your pay rates are keeping up with the market. Your strategy will need to allow for adjusting pay rate increases to keep aligned with the market.

Another option is to lead the market. This means you will set a pay rate higher than the market. By doing this, you increase the number of qualified job seekers and decrease employee turnover. This option is widely used for companies faced with the war for talent that we discussed in the earlier chapter where there is a shortage of qualified job seekers.

Another reason for adopting this philosophy is that employees will be less likely to leave your company for pay reasons. However, the downside to this approach is that this strategy leads to an increase in your labor cost and you will need to monitor whether you are realizing these benefits.

You may also decide to establish pay rates below the market. This is referred to as *lag the market*. Some companies simply do not have the resources to pay at the same rate of the market.

This could cause a decrease in qualified job seekers. However, you can supplement your compensation program to include perks and benefits that are attractive. This strategy is effective where job seekers are not focused on the pay, rather on the entire compensation package. One of the companies I worked with always paid below the market, but made up for it in employee medical benefits, company culture, and employee-development programs. They also implemented a bonus program tied to the overall success of the company. Therefore, when the company profited, so did the employees without jeopardizing the company's financial position by having a large, fixed labor cost.

You may decide to implement a combination of options. For example, you may choose to lead the market during a tight labor market, and change your philosophy as the market changes. You may select key positions where you want to lead the market and others where you will match the market. Regardless of what you choose, the most important factor is to keep current on compensation trends so you can adjust accordingly. The last thing you want is to wake up one day and realize your employee turnover rate has significantly increased due to an imbalance in one of your key compensation components.

What defines your compensation strategy? There are many considerations of a compensation strategy to use when developing your compensation package. The first is budget. Work with your financial partner to develop the amount of money you can spend on salaries and benefits. Meet with your employee benefit broker to obtain market research on benefit allocations for companies similar to your size and industry.

Next, develop salary ranges for each position. Review the pay rate for each employee on your payroll. Below is an example of the information you need to collect.

- Employee
- Position
- Payrate
- Date of Hire

- Years Experience
- Education, Special Skills, Credentials

During this process, you should identify if you have any internal pay equity issues. In other words, do you have employees who have similar positions but are getting paid differently? If so, is there a specific reason why? Perhaps some have more experience with your company or more skills than others? It is common to find you have a few pay equity issues and will need to adjust accordingly.

The next step is to review salary information in the market by use of salary and pay internet sites to determine average salaries in your geographical area. You can then determine these ranges as noted in the example below.

Position	Minimum Pay Rate	Maximum Pay Rate
Accountant I	$40,000	$45,000
Accountant II	$45,000	$55,000
Receptionist	$38,000	$44,000

Other factors to consider for your compensation package include both cash and noncash compensation. Non-monetary compensation can include many different elements and can comprise 20-50% of the value of the cash compensation an employee receives. Below is a list of examples of cash and noncash benefits employees may receive in addition to their pay.

Cash Benefits

- Employee medical benefits (health, dental, vision, life insurance)

- Paid time off or vacation
- Holidays
- 401k contributions
- Profit sharing, bonus, and/or commission pay
- Volunteer paid time off
- Family and/or parental leave
- Car or vehicle allowance
- Cell phone allowance
- Education reimbursement

Non-Cash Benefits

- Flexible work schedule
- Working from home options
- Private office space versus a cubicle or an office with a window
- Career-development opportunities and training programs
- Casual dress code
- Employee-engagement opportunities such as involvement in important projects
- Volunteer program without pay
- Special equipment (new laptop computer or cell phone)
- Symbolic rewards (Employee of the month, top performer)

Like the research you did to compare salaries in the market, you will want to compare your benefits against those offered by other companies of your size and industry. If you are a start-up company, you may also want to learn what other start-up companies are offering. You can obtain this information from professional organizations within your industry and by asking others on various social media and internet sites. Again, decide if you want to lead, match, or lag the market with your benefit offerings.

Keep in mind what is important to one employee regarding your compensation package may greatly differ with another. Millennials, for example, may be more concerned with opportunities to grow and learn than they are with just pay. Generation X may be concerned with flexible work schedules and volunteerism. Baby Boomers may be concerned with retirement, medical benefits, and economic stability. Make sure you monitor the pulse of what is important to your workforce and spend your money accordingly.

When developing a compensation strategy, you will need to make sure that it is legally compliant with the Department of Labor (DOL) Fair Labor Standards Act (FLSA). Factors to consider may include minimum wage, overtime pay, or gender equity pay as defined by the Lilly Ledbetter Fair Pay act. As we discussed earlier in this chapter, if you have any internal pay equity issues, resolve them immediately, and make sure there are no disparities between protected classes (gender, race, age).

Communicating to job candidates and employees about your company's compensation package is important for both recruiting and retention. The direct and indirect costs of compensation are significant. Employees may not realize the value of the entire compensation package unless you are clear about communicating its value. Creating a compensation report for each employee may be useful to show them the benefits. One of the companies I worked with asked a recently departed employee why he resigned.

The employee responded it was because he was offered a higher salary. As the employee explained what his offer included, the manager quickly realized that although this employee thought he was getting a pay raise, his total compensation package was much less. He had forgotten to consider his annual bonus which allocated an additional 15% of his base pay.

EMPLOYEE COMPENSATION STATEMENT

YOUR TOTAL OVERALL COMPENSATION PACKAGE:

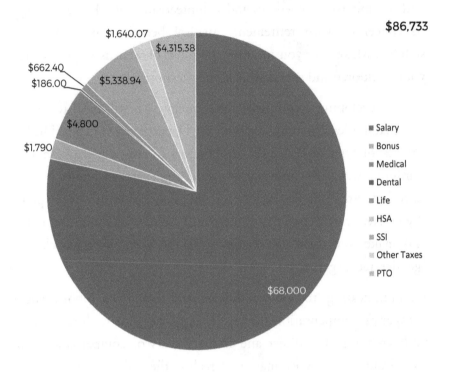

$86,733

Salary	$	68,000.00
Bonus	$	1,790.00
Medical	$	4,800.00
Dental	$	186.00
Life	$	662.40
HSA	$	-
SSI	$	5,338.94
Other Taxes	$	1,640.07
PTO	$	4,315.38

This story illustrates why I recommend creating a summary of the employee's compensation annually to distribute to employees (as indicated in the example provided on the previous page). Although the base pay for this employee is $68,000, the overall compensation package is $86,733. No two companies provide the exact benefit offerings and therefore the values differ significantly.

When it comes to employee compensation, one of the most frequently asked questions I get is about transparency with employees regarding your compensation strategy. Typically, the more transparent you are with your compensation strategy, the more trust you will build with your employees, potentially avoiding trouble in the future. More and more companies share with their employees the pay salary ranges for positions within their company. Now, this doesn't mean that you disclose what an individual earns, only the salary range for positions within your company.

Transparency also leads to increased employee-engagement. You can use this information to encourage employees to advance in your company. By doing this, the employee will see the pay increase at the next pay level and may work to acquire the skills and performance level required to advance.

Another question many employers ask is whether they can prohibit employees from discussing compensation among each other. For the most part, the answer is no. Effective April 2014, President Barack Obama signed an executive order protecting employees for companies covered by the National Labor Relations Act. If you want to include a policy prohibiting employees from discussing pay, my advice is to seek an employment attorney for further discussion.

EXERCISE:
Compensation Strategy

Now that you understand what you should consider when developing a compensation strategy, you are ready to construct a compensation plan that will support your business objectives. The following questions and activities are designed to help you with this process.

Which of the following is your pay philosophy?

- Match the Market
- Lead the Market
- Lag the Market

SALARY SCHEDULE

Create a salary schedule that includes positions and pay information. The next series of exercises are examples of how to identify job families, rank positions, and determine pay ranges for the positions. Your company size and number of positions will determine how detailed you need this process. I will present various examples of this process. Review the level of detail involved with each and select the best processes for your company

LIST OF POSITIONS

Create a spreadsheet that lists the positions in your company. You may decide, depending on the size of your company, to group positions into job families. For example, administrative, technical, finance, sales, and marketing.

Job Positions	Job Family
Receptionist	Administrative
Administrative Assistant	Administrative
Office Manager/HR	Administrative
Director of Operations Manager	Administrative
Accounts Payable Clerk	Finance
Accountant	Finance
Controller	Finance
Customer Service/Relations Representative	Sales and Marketing
Sales Representative	Sales and Marketing
Marketing Coordinator	Sales and Marketing
Sales and Marketing Manager	Sales and Marketing

Another example of how job families might be grouped would be non-management jobs, technical jobs, management jobs, and executive jobs. You may also choose to group positions by geographic locations if you employ in multiple cities or states.

RANKING JOB POSITIONS

Next you may want to rank the jobs based on the job complexity, job worth and/or level of responsibility. This process involves comparing the job duties and requirements to other jobs within your company. There are two ways you can rank jobs:

One is to assign points to each job based on specific criteria. The more points assigned to a job, the more worth the job is to the company. Jobs worth more are assigned a higher pay.

The second way you can rank the jobs is simpler and involves rank ordering the value or worth of each job in comparison to the other jobs within the same job family. This method is frequently used in smaller companies. Below is an example of this ranking.

Job Positions	Job Family	Ranking
Receptionist	Administrative	1
Administrative Assistant	Administrative	2
Office Manager/HR	Administrative	3
Director of Operations Manager	Administrative	4
Accounts Payable Clerk	Finance	1
Accountant	Finance	2
Senior Accountant	Finance	3
Controller	Finance	4
Customer Service/Relations Representative	Sales and Marketing	1
Sales Representative	Sales and Marketing	2
Marketing Coordinator	Sales and Marketing	3
Sales and Marketing Manager	Sales and Marketing	4

CONDUCTING SALARY RESEARCH

Now you are ready to research salary and pay information for each of your positions. When doing this make sure the job responsibilities match your positions, not just the title. For example, at one company, my title was Vice President of Human Resources, but my job duties and the structure of the HR department better aligned with the job title of Human Resource Manager.

CREATING PAY GRADES

When conducting market research, you can obtain this information from professional organizations, resources through internet searches, and the Bureau of Labor Statistics. You will discover that the market information related to pay is often organized in pay ranges. You may want to create pay grades for each position. If you don't have many positions within your company, you may choose to omit creating pay grades and only create pay ranges instead. Use market data to group positions based on similar salary survey data.

A start-up or small organization might have only three or four pay grades. The federal government, by contrast, uses 15 pay grades. Below is an example of how you would organize your data for establishing six pay grades within your company.

Grade 1	Grade 2	Grade 3	Grade 4	Grade 5	Grade 6
Receptionist	Accountant	Senior Accountant	Accounting Manager	Controller	CFO
Accounts Payable Clerk	Administrative Assistant	Senior Administrative Assistant	Office Manager/ HR	Director of Operations Manager	COO
Customer Service/ Relations Representative	Sales Representative	Marketing Coordinator	Sales and Marketing Manager	Director of Sales	CEO

CREATING PAY RANGES

Employers can group positions having similar market pay ranges together into the same pay grade. For example, a Grade One position may have a pay range of $15 to $20 per hour and a Grade Two position may have a pay range from $18 to $24 per hour. An employer can have as many or as few pay grades as it wants.

Even if you do not create pay grades, you can create pay ranges for your positions. You can determine these internally, but most companies use the market information to identify percentiles and then develop the ranges accordingly. For example, you may want to consider a midpoint of a pay range to be 50th percentile to meet the market. If your company's philosophy is to lead the market, the salary point will be above the 50th percentile for most positions.

To create the pay ranges, you need to create a minimum, midpoint, and maximum point. Most companies implement a 30% or 40% range. Below are two formulas you may elect to use when creating your pay ranges.

The formulas for a 30% range using the midpoint as the base are:

- Maximum = Midpoint x 1.15
- Minimum = Midpoint x 0.85

The formulas for a 40% range when the midpoint is known are:

- Maximum = Midpoint x 1.20
- Minimum = Midpoint x 0.80

Each job family can have its own pay grades and pay ranges that are established independently from the other job families. Here is an example of a few job grades based on a 40% range:

Proposed Ranges	Min	Mid	Max
Grade I	$10.40	$13.00	$15.60
Receptionist	(market salary = $13.00)		
Accounts Payable Clerk	(market salary = $14.00)		
Grade II	$14.20	$17.75	$21.30
Administrative Assistant	(market salary = $17.50)		
Sales Representative	(market salary = $18.00)		

Add this information in your salary schedule as indicated below:

Job Positions	Min	Mid	Max
Receptionist	$10.40 per hour	$13.00 per hour	$15.60 per hour
Administrative Assistant	$14.20 per hour	$17.75 per hour	$21.30 per hour
Office Manager/HR	$17.60 per hour	$22.00 per hour	$26.40 per hour
Director of Operations Manager	$60,000	$75,000	$90,000

Document the pay rate for each of your employees. Now you are ready to add a column for the employee name to the salary schedule. Once completed you should have a clear representation of each person's pay, position, and the accommodating pay range you have developed. Below is an example of the company's salary schedule.

Employee Name	Job Positions	Current Pay	Low	Mid-Range	High
S. Smith	Receptionist	$15.00 per hour	$12.80 per hour	$16.00 per hour	$19.20 per hour
L. Harman	Administrative Assistant	$18.00 per hour	$14.40 per hour	$18.00 per hour	$21.60 per hour
M. Trevino	Administrative Assistant	$18.50 per hour			
M. Nguyen	Office Manager/HR	$25.00 per hour	$17.60 per hour	$22.00 per hour	$26.40 per hour
H. Taylor	Director of Operations Manager	$72,000	$60,000	$75,000	$90,000

You can also add columns that include date of hire, education, special designations and/or years of experience in the industry. These additional areas can help you identify equity issues related to pay or help you determine reasons and justification for paying people different pay rates.

BENEFITS

Select the benefits that your company offers or would like to offer by checking the boxes from the list below.

Cash Benefits

☐ Employee medical benefits (health, dental, vision, life insurance)
☐ Paid time off or vacation
☐ Holidays
☐ 401k contributions
☐ Profit sharing, bonus and/or commission pay
☐ Volunteer paid time off

☐ Family and/or parental leave
☐ Car or vehicle allowance
☐ Cell phone allowance
☐ Education Reimbursement
☐ Other

Non-Cash Benefits

☐ Flexible work schedule
☐ Working from home options
☐ Private office space versus a cubicle or an office with a window
☐ Career-development opportunities and training programs
☐ Casual dress code
☐ Employee-engagement opportunities such as involvement in important projects
☐ Volunteer program without pay
☐ Special equipment (new laptop computer or cell phone)
☐ Symbolic rewards (Employee of the month, top performer)
☐ Other:

Compensation Package Summary

Do you want to create compensation package summaries to distribute to employees?

Yes

No

Your total compensation package can be a valuable recruiting and retention tool. Make sure you communicate the value of your compensation package to prospective employees. Use this information when pitching to the job candidates.

CONCLUSION

Whether you are an established, emerging, or start-up company, defining your compensation strategy is critical to your financial success. Without a clear direction, you might find yourself unnecessarily paying over the market, which might jeopardize your financial stability. You might only need to track your employee pay internally to monitor the pulse on pay equity issues or employee retention issues related to compensation. As your company grows and the number of positions increase, then a formalized compensation schedule with pay grades and ranking becomes necessary.

CHAPTER FOUR

RECRUITING STARTS WITH THE END IN MIND

THE RIGHT SOURCE METHOD

As mentioned in Chapter Two, The Right Source Method is a combination of recruiting strategies and hiring processes I developed that include processes and techniques to improve your hiring results. These strategies are outlined in this chapter and Chapter Five, The Hiring Process.

Recruiting is more than filling vacancies or, pardon the expression, *putting butts in seats.*

When determining your recruiting strategy, begin with the end in mind. Most hiring managers focus on the basics, such as the type of experience and skills needed to perform the job duties. A strategic manager thinks on a deeper level and asks, "What type of personality traits and behaviors attribute to success on the job and success in my company culture?"

> When determining your recruiting strategy, begin with the end in mind.

How does one go about finding the answers to these questions? It is not an easy task. That is why recruiting firms charge the fees they do, because the process can be daunting and difficult.

I have always loved recruiting. Probably because I relate recruiting to sales. The process is somewhat similar. Sales is about first listening to customers and determining their needs, then marketing the service or product to the customer. When conversing with the hiring manager, I first find out about the needs of the company by asking a series of questions. What is the single most important attribute to success on the job? Or in some cases, what failures have they encountered during the selection process? Or, what challenges have people faced in this position?

In recruiting the work is not done yet because you must also determine the needs of the candidates. Why is the candidate looking for a new position? What is important to them in the next job? Is it pay, job security, or the work environment? There is always a dominant factor driving them to change jobs or factors that influence their decision to accept a new position.

I sometimes ask candidates, "What would cause you to leave this position later if you are selected to work at this company?" When trying to determine which candidate is the best fit, I collect this information from both parties and then base my selection accordingly. In other words, how does the manager envision success in the role? And if selected, what will it take for the candidate to be happy in this role?

IS RECRUITING AN ART OR A SCIENCE?

Some people consider recruiting an art and others perceive it more of a science. I believe recruiting is both of those things. Some people have a gift for selecting great people. I think that comes from being greatly attuned to everything one observes during the process and absorbing the information needed to identify the top talent. This process involves looking at what is behind the resume. Like an artist who embraces the beauty of nature and transfers that beauty onto the canvas, this is a gift of talent. A highly exceptional recruiter has the same type of talent—the ability to select and pair top talent, as well as the ability to eliminate those not so good.

On the other hand, there is a science to the recruiting process as well. The science of recruiting refers to using technology, systems, and instruments to discover attributes, personality traits, experiences, and skills that predict a good hire. These processes can be helpful in collecting information that improves the selection process. It includes analyzing hiring trends based on your recruitment as well as benchmarking talent. There are sophisticated technology systems and analytic tools you can use to accomplish this, but for smaller companies simply collecting information from a variety of sources can provide much insight. You can collect information by conducting exit interviews, which can help you evaluate your company culture and understand employee lifestyle preferences. You should also consider how effective you and your managers are in communicating with and engaging employees.

Also, reviewing employee information such as the types of companies (size and culture) and educational background (large or small university and types of degrees) can often indicate trends leading to better selection.

At one of my former companies, a small professional services firm, we avoided recruiting from large universities because most of the students were from larger urban areas and were seeking employment in larger cities and with larger firms. Our firm was small and consisted of several small branch locations in small towns. Therefore, our ideal candidate was someone who preferred to work for a smaller organization and was often someone from a smaller community who would thrive in a small-town, close-knit environment.

Your supervisors can also provide valuable information related to successful hiring practices. Begin by asking them to describe their top talent and why they are a good fit for the position. Ask if there are specific personality traits or skills that are essential for success on the job. Be careful to evaluate the relevance and legality of this information. I once worked with a hiring manager who determined whether she would hire a person based on how fast they walked beside her. Her theory was that if they were a slow walker, they would not keep up with the workload.

Keep in mind that all criteria and processes must be legally defendable. What does that mean? You must maintain a legal hiring process that includes interview questions and criteria related to the job and that are not discriminatory. In this case, someone who had a physical disability (or an older employee) that impaired their ability to walk fast would be discriminated against. And the relevance of this test to the job duties could not be defended.

Another example of illegal hiring practices is asking questions about whether a candidate has children. This is considered discriminatory as you may be concerned that someone with small children may have attendance issues. Questions related to children, age, citizenship, criminal records, disability, race, marital status, housing, and military status are common areas where employers can expose themselves to liability risk.

Begin with the end in mind relates to two areas: workforce planning and selection. Workforce planning can be a complex process involving analyzing your current workforce and determining gaps in employee talent areas. Let's keep it simple and focus on workforce planning as a process of identifying your hiring needs and determining when you need to start the selection process.

What you want to avoid is waiting until you are understaffed or in a bind and forced to hire someone quickly. I have witnessed a hiring manager more concerned with filling a vacancy as fast as possible instead of focusing on selecting the right person.

As you develop your business plan for the year, or even for the quarter, it is essential that you identify when you anticipate hiring for either a new or a replacement position. Once you have decided to include these positions in your workforce, you need to estimate the time it will take you to fill the position.

EXERCISE
Forecast and Develop Your Workforce Plan

Begin by forecasting when you anticipate hiring certain positions. You may want to look back at the previous year and review hiring trends as well as review your company growth plan to determine future positions. For example, one of my former companies issued an annual bonus in March. Every year we would see an increase in turnover in April after employees received this bonus. The employees were waiting until they received the bonus before they resigned.

Include vacancies and new hires in this process. If you are launching a new service or product, determine which positions you will need associated with that task. Once these positions have been identified, you need to determine how long you anticipate it will take to hire the best candidate. Again, look at your hiring trends in the past.

Typically, the more technical and specialized the position, the longer this process can take. Supply and demand also contributes to the length of time it takes to fill a position. As you can see in the example below, if you need to hire a sales representative in January, and it takes about six weeks to fill the position, begin recruiting in mid-November.

Month	Need to Hire	Time to Fill	Begin to Recruit
January	Sales	60 days	November
	Customer Service	30 days	December
April	Engineer	45 days	February

Now that you have forecast your hiring needs, it is time to develop a plan to recruit and select the best talent. This is the second part of *begin with the end in mind*. The Right Source Method includes a successful selection process to locate and select the best candidate. Simply posting a job and sorting through resumes without a clear process will most likely result in a poor selection. To help you develop a strategic recruiting plan, I have included questions that will guide you through the right sourcing process.

THE BASICS

The first part of the Right Source Method is simple: Determine the basic requirements of the job. Requirements will include the skills, knowledge, and abilities (SKA) needed to complete the roles and responsibilities of the job successfully. Review the job description to acquire this information or create a list of the primary job duties and identify the SKAs, past experiences, and education requirements needed to perform the job duties. Below is a sample of the basic information you will need to screen applicants for an administrative assistant:

Primary job duties include managing the office administrative tasks, such as answering phones, maintaining necessary supplies, creating documents, corresponding with clients and associates on behalf of management, reconciling expense reports, and managing travel calendars. The Candidate needs 3-5 years of administrative experience and sound knowledge of Microsoft Office, especially Outlook, Word, and Power Point.

As you receive applications, use this information to screen and sort through the first round of candidates. When you call candidates and screen them, your questions will address the basics. This is where most interviewers stop. They try to select the strongest candidate by determining who meets the basic job requirements.

To improve your selection process, you need to consider other information which will help you predict how the candidate will assimilate with your group and succeed in their new role. Create and use a candidate profile to achieve this. Let's review this process in more detail.

THE CANDIDATE PROFILE

Candidate profiles provide you insight into traits and skills that are common among top talent. These profiles can also be used to educate your hiring managers who will participate with the selection process. This may seem like a lot of trouble, but the more information you have, the better your results.

To create a candidate profile, begin by asking this question to yourself and others, "If you were to describe the perfect candidate in regard to their personality traits, work style preferences, and background, what would this look like?"

When reviewing work experience, consider whether they have experience performing the job duties and consider the size and type of companies where they have worked. As discussed earlier, the size and type of company can predict the potential for job success, but the structure of the reporting infrastructure can also be helpful. One of my companies preferred recruiting administrative assistants who had worked directly for the owner of the company as opposed to working in a larger company. They found that previous hires from larger companies had difficulty working in an entrepreneurial environment where things were constantly changing. Another client, an insurance brokerage, preferred selecting candidates from smaller brokerages instead of large insurance carriers because of the differences they found in a candidate's customer service values.

Another example of expanding beyond the basics pertains to education requirements. I once worked with a small manufacturing company that recruited recent college graduates for entry-level marketing positions. We targeted smaller universities because we could attract qualified candidates seeking an opportunity to gain experience. In these institutions candidates were typically more flexible in their salary requirements and aligned better with the pay structure of the small company.

Creating a candidate profile also includes determining the traits and characteristics your employees need to have that align with your company's mission, core values, and operation goals. Below is a sample of a candidate profile for an executive assistant that expands beyond the basic requirements.

Candidate must be a self-starter with a high level of initiative where he/she works independently and without much direction. The Candidate must have a professional and friendly demeanor when speaking on the phone and in communicating with others. The Candidate should demonstrate a strong trait of attention to detail. Experience working in a smaller organization is preferred where expectations are to wear many hats and the work environment is fast-paced.

When developing your candidate profile. Ask key employees, managers, or supervisors how they would describe the perfect candidate. Ask them to evaluate their best employees, identify their traits and past experiences, and education.

Determine the dynamics of the workgroup and management to identify the personality type that would succeed in that environment. Sometimes it is easier to determine what to avoid. For example, someone who needs a lot of direction and supervision may not be able to resolve complex problems and work in an environment that requires initiative and problem solving.

So how do you determine whether the candidate fits the profile? You develop a set of questions that relate to the traits and experiences you identified when creating the candidate profile. These types of questions are considered behavioral questions. Behavioral interview questions are designed to solicit responses from candidates that indicate if they have demonstrated this trait in the past. The concept is that past experiences predict future success. For example, "Tell me about a time when you saw something that was not working in your organization." This question will encourage a candidate to discuss past work experience in a way that will help you determine if they can identify an issue and take initiative to improve or change the situation they describe.

Asking questions about their previous work environment, such as, "How would you describe your preferred work environment?" will help you determine the type of management and work environment they prefer.

These questions elicit better responses than simply asking, "Tell me about your work experience at ABC Company." Interviewing involves skills and techniques that are developed over time, and always includes a set of good questions.

EXERCISE

Now that you are forming a deeper understanding of what makes a great candidate, let's work through an exercise that will help you develop this process. In the example below, the first column includes a list of behaviors associated with success on the job. The right column contains the traits related to these requirements. A list of traits can be found on our website www.premierhrsolutions.net.

Job and Profile Requirements	Traits Needed
Company value—Service	Customer Service
Company value—Integrity	Integrity
Self-Starter	Initiative
Ability to work alone	Autonomy
Fast-paced environment	Flexibility

In this section, identify a position in your company. Next list the job requirements and then the trait that will help you determine whether they will be able to fulfill the requirement successfully.

Name of Position:	
Job and Profile Requirements	Traits Needed

Once you have completed this exercise, you need to create a set of behavioral interview questions associated with each trait. Identify situations that highlight the traits or qualities you are seeking. For example, employees with great customer service typically go above and beyond what is expected to satisfy a customer. A question related to this would be, "Describe a situation where you went above and beyond to satisfy a customer." Someone who is attentive to detail has a process for checking their work for accuracy. A question related to this would be, "How do you ensure the accuracy of your work?" Ask your managers and key employees to help you with this process. Those in the trenches can relate to what is necessary to excel in these roles.

Next you will need to determine the response that demonstrates strength in this trait. Vague answers such as "I do that all the time," without giving an example typically does not demonstrate strength. You can ask follow-up questions such as, "Can you elaborate?", but avoid prompting the candidate too much. Those who have strength in the trait will naturally respond with their own examples and work habits. I usually benchmark successful responses by asking top talent within the organization to answer these questions, and by collecting responses and comparing these to successful hires.

Behavioral interview questions can be found through researching the internet and through books and articles. You may want to invest in some training as well. HR consultants can help you develop and perfect your interviews, bench mark top talent in your organization, and train you and your hiring team. The next table is an example of this process:

Job and Profile Requirements	Traits Needed	Interview Questions
Company values — Service	Customer Service	Tell me about a time that you went above and beyond to satisfy a customer.
Company values — Integrity	Integrity	What would you do if someone asked you to do something unethical?
Self-Starter	Initiative	Give me an example of an important goal that you had set in the past.
Ability to work alone	Autonomy	When taking on a new task, do you like to have a great deal of feedback and responsibility at the outset, or do you like to try your own approach?
Fast-paced environment	Flexibility	What do you do when priorities change quickly? Give me one example of when this happened.

Equally important in this process is to consider your bad hires and determine trends in poor hiring selection. For example, factors like length of commute to work was affecting our retention rates with one company. In another company, we realized we were hiring overly qualified applicants which resulted in these candidates leaving after several months, because they became bored in their new position and left to pursue other opportunities. Since we were not giving them enough challenge, they were quickly dissatisfied and sought more fulfilling roles. In this situation, we switched our strategy to seeking candidates who met the job requirements and had a strong desire to be trained. We began looking at less experienced candidates who were quick learners who we could develop and promote over time.

As simple as it sounds, your take away here is to remember when evaluating candidates, it is important to ask yourself if it makes sense for the candidate to work in this role instead of simply considering whether they can perform the job duties. For example, an executive assistant can most likely fulfill a receptionist duty. But does that seem like the best fit?

THE SUCCESS FACTORS:

Finally, as you finish this process of determining the best fit for the position, take a few minutes to determine success factors. What does success look like after 30, 60, or 90 days on the job? In other words, if you were to evaluate the new hire to determine if it was a good hire, what factors will you consider when determining success?

Why are we considering this so early in the process? This is important because it forces you to consider success factors that you can identify in the candidates when making your selection. An example of determining success may be attendance. The employee's ability to perform their job duties successfully will be jeopardized if they are consistently absent. Therefore, reviewing a person's job history and asking questions regarding their attendance or why they left their last jobs may reveal if there is a problem in this area. The ability to work collaboratively within a team may also be a success factor, so asking questions related to working within a team would be helpful. In the next exercise are examples of success factors to consider for new hires. When evaluating candidates ask yourself which of these are most important and does the candidate demonstrate these traits?

EXERCISE:

Attendance and punctuality – Being on time and punctual demonstrates commitment to the company and the team. It can be viewed as a sign of respect to others as well.

Teamwork – The ability to work well with others both within the department and across departments may be essential to certain positions.

Positive attitude – Maintaining a positive attitude during the transition of a new position is key to assimilating within an organization. A positive attitude is a sign of strong emotional intelligence.

Willingness to learn – The first six months of a job is consumed with learning opportunities and being open to learning the procedures set by an organization and new ways of performing certain job duties. It is most likely instrumental to success in many positions.

Dependability and accountability – The ability to develop trust and confidence from the manager and the team when delivering on assignments and completing tasks.

Customer-service values – Having a customer service mentality that matches your company's core values.

Problem solving – The ability to figure things out on their own may be critical if your company doesn't provide a thorough training process.

Company culture – The ability to understand and embrace the company culture and deal with company politics and the structure of the organization.

Communication skills – This includes the ability to communicate effectively and knowing when it is best to speak out and when not.

List and describe the top three factors you will consider when evaluating whether you made a good hire.

Success Factors	Describe what this looks like:
1.	
2.	
3.	

CONCLUSION

You should now have a deeper understanding of the process entailed when developing a successful recruiting strategy. Equally important is to understand that each company's culture, people, and infrastructure will be unique, which leads to different recruiting strategies from company to company. Recruiting strategies may differ with each position as well. Taking the time to describe top talent and success on the job and determining criteria for evaluating candidates will greatly increase your success in hiring.

CHAPTER FIVE

THE HIRING PROCESS

Now that you have a deeper understanding of recruiting with the end in mind, let's discuss the basics of the recruitment process. In this chapter, we will review the overall recruitment process and most importantly explain *The Funnel Approach,* which is part of the Right Source Method. I have developed and found this approach to provide exceptional results when transitioning candidates through the process. If you take the time and effort to follow these steps, you will make an informed decision, thus improving your selection results. The recruitment process includes four primary actions as noted in the figure below:

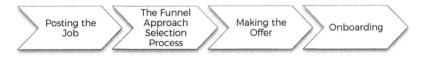

The job description must be created first and then posted in such a way that it will both attract attention and bring results in the form of applicants. You have two objectives when creating and posting the job description. One is that first impressions are important. You want your job posting to reflect a good impression of your company and create interest in the position. Secondly, your job posting needs to be successful attracting qualified candidates. To achieve these two objectives, follow these three primary guidelines:

- Create a Job Title that is search engine friendly. The first two words need to match terms that job seekers are searching. For example, your company may refer to the receptionist as The Director of First Impression, but job seekers will be searching for receptionist. If you are unsure what to title the position, log onto the website of the job board where you will post and search as if you were a candidate. This will give you great insight into what your target audience is seeking and allow you to match their criteria to your job posting.

- Write the post as if it is an advertisement. Just like advertisements are intended to sell something, your intent is to influence job candidates to come work for your company. You should identify your target audience, address them in the language they understand, and highlight features they will find attractive. Think about why this is a good job and showcase your company and the benefits for coming to work for you. Include the job's main requirements and finish with a strong call to action like, "Apply today to join our great team!" This may seem like a lot of effort, but a strong job posting recruits better candidates. Include the information you developed when creating your recruiting pitch from Chapter Two.

- Be clear but concise. When it comes to the job description, you need to include the most important job duties and requirements, but not necessarily list everything. Good job descriptions are usually 300 to 800 words in length. Start with a one- or two-sentence overview of the position, followed by benefits of working for your company and finish with the preferred qualifications or requirements for the job. As you write the job description, remember to use compelling key words. Nolan Gray, author of *5 Tips for Crafting More Effective Job Postings* says it best, "Tired language like, A qualified candidate will demonstrate ... will make most candidates yawn. Instead, consider more compelling phrases like, fearless critical thinker or passionate believer in... ."

If you are not receiving qualified candidates, you probably need to rewrite your job posting and post it again. I recall one position we recruited that was a commission-pay contractor position. Although we received many applicants, we struggled to attract candidates who were truly interested in this position. We revised the job posting several times until we found the right verbiage to attract applicants who met our profile.

Now that you have a dynamic job posting created, the next step is to determine where to post the job. Using the candidate profile you developed, identify the audience you will draw from to find this candidate. Where will they be searching for jobs? What job boards attract this audience? Your choice will depend on broad variables, including your industry, the type of position, the experience needed, job specialty, and generation.

There are many places to post your jobs. The most traditional are employment job boards, such as Monster, Career Builder, Glassdoor, and Indeed. I have found Craig's List to be successful for entry level, trade positions, and retail positions. This process will require trial and error as well. Below are some other places to post jobs:

- Professional organizations and associations for professions such as Certified Public Accountants, HR Management, Nurses, Engineers
- University Alumni Associations
- College career job boards
- Industry trade associations (medical, manufacturing)
- LinkedIn groups related to professions and industry
- Job Seeker networks, both online and meetups
- Internally post your job through your company email inviting employees to refer others to apply
- Social Media (LinkedIn, Facebook and Blogs where candidates may be visiting)
- Your company website

Job posting cost can be expensive. I recommend you track your results for the places you post. Include the cost, the number of candidates that you attract, the number of qualified candidates, and the number you hired. I would also include the name of the person hired so that you can further evaluate success on the job at a later date. Keep track of the referral source of each hire so you can determine best hiring trends. This will include which job board the candidate was sourced from, and employee referrals, resume searches, and networking. An example of how to track this information is presented in the table on the next page.

Position	Administrative Assistant	Inside Sales
Job Posting Source	FindYourNext Job.com	Your Company Website
Cost	$300 per 30-day posting	$0
# of candidates	75	15
# qualified	25	3
Days to Fill	30	60
Employee	Mary Smith	John Henry

One other technique for locating candidates is by conducting searches through resume databases. This technique is a time-consuming process and is often better implemented by professional recruiters who have the search tools and resources to conduct these effectively. Most of the job boards have a resume database that allows you to create searches. You can also create alerts on these sites that send you notifications when a new job seeker has posted their resume that meets your search criteria.

THE FUNNEL APPROACH

Now that you have created a dynamic job posting and advertised in various locations to attract top talent, how will you manage the large number of candidates that a great job posting generates? In today's market, finding the right candidate can be overwhelming due to the sheer volume of job seekers and the daunting process it takes to wade through the applicant pool. I find it useful to go beyond the basic screening and interview process. I refer to this as the funnel approach and although it takes more time upfront, your success rate will increase significantly in the long run.

Your funnel will have a large number of candidates at the top. Use the funnel selection process to narrow the application pool until there are only a few candidates. In essence, you look for more than an applicant to fill a position; you look for the best match for the position and the company.

Here is what the Funnel Approach looks like:

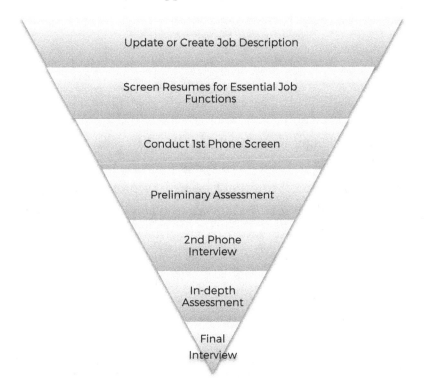

Screen Resumes for Essential Job Requirements
Conduct 1st phone interview
Preliminary Assessment
2nd phone interview
In-depth Assessment
Final Interview

The Funnel Approach screens resumes according to the essential qualifications that a candidate must have before proceeding to the next step in the interview process. Although the process is comprehensive, it is meant to move quickly. In most cases, you should be able to move a candidate through this process in about a week. If your process is too slow, you may lose qualified candidates to other employers in the market. The goal is to narrow the immense number of candidates down to a final few through a systematic approach based on best practices. Once you have received a resume you need to act upon it immediately and move candidates through this process.

In the previous chapter, we discussed creating a list of the basic job requirements for each open position. This list includes the technical skills required, work history, experience level, and education requirements. You must select the must-haves from this list. For example, when recruiting for an Executive Assistant we were searching for at least 5 years of EA experience and determined that their most current position must be an EA role.

Most candidates met the technical job requirements. We could then quickly sort through the applicant pool by looking at the job seeker's most current position and eliminating those who were not in an EA role. We also were seeking a candidate who had worked directly for the owner of a business but found that this would narrow our candidate pool too much and therefore decided not to eliminate these candidates.

After selecting the candidates who meet the basic requirements, you need to store these candidates in a pipeline. Recruiting companies and large companies often have applicant tracking software that allows them to upload resumes and link them to positions and document where they are in the hiring process. However, you can manage these by saving them in electronic folders and creating your own pipeline as seen below.

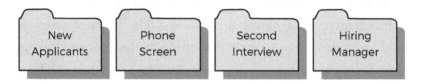

Now screen the resumes and reject those that don't meet these basic requirements. The resume screening should only take a minute or so per resume. Don't waste time reading through the entire resume if the candidate does not readily meet the minimum criteria.

The phone screen is the next step of the process and consists of a 10- to 15-minute phone interview where you will review the applicant's job history and qualifications with the candidate. You will also want to briefly discuss the job duties and a couple of key behavioral questions that provide a preliminary insight to personality traits. I always ask about salary requirements at this first call because you don't want to move a candidate through the process only to find out at the end that you cannot meet their salary requirements. Sometimes candidates may be reluctant to give their salary requirements and I will not proceed until I have at least some salary history. I inform them that salary is negotiated at the final stage, but it is important not to waste anyone's time at this point. If you have a predetermined pay rate that cannot be negotiated, then inform them at this point in the event they want to withdraw their consideration. It is important to note here to check your state employment regulations for asking job candidates about previous salary history. In some states it is unlawful to do so.

I advise using knockout questions in the early part of the phone screen. A knockout question might be something like, "What are your salary requirements?" or "What is your experience in …?" If the candidate does not provide the required response, then you discontinue the interview to save time.

For some positions, you might want to include a first-level assessment that includes technical testing such as computer, math, cognitive, or industry knowledge skills. At this point you can eliminate some candidates and prepare for the second round of interviewing.

In the second phone interview, you should expect to allocate 30 minutes for your interview and include the behavioral interview questions you created for the position.

For both the phone screen and second interview, it is important to create an interview template you can use to record their responses and take notes. This is important so that you can effectively compare candidates. You should follow the same process consistently with all candidates for the best results. Below is a sample of an interview template:

Interviewer:	Date:
Candidate:	

Thank you for coming in to speak with me today. The purpose of our meeting is to show you around our facility and finish the interview process. This is not necessarily your typical interview. I will ask you some behavioral and situational questions, so I can get a better understanding of your thoughts and the way you work.	
Describe the position and ask, "Tell me about your work experience and how it relates to this position."	
Do you consider yourself a positive person? Please explain.	
Describe your "ideal" job. Or What is going to make you happiest in a job?	
In your opinion, what are the key ingredients for guiding and maintaining successful relationships with others at work?	
How would your coworkers describe you? Can you explain?	
Why are you interested in this position?	
What questions do you have for me? (explain next steps of the process and when you anticipate making a decision.	

After the second interview, you should have final candidates who you want to schedule for face-to-face interviews with the hiring manager. At this point, some companies choose to administer an in-depth assessment, which evaluates mental and emotional intelligence and identifies personality traits that you might have overlooked in the selection process. Pre-employment assessments have proven to be successful in reducing turnover in companies by improving the selection process. There are a variety of assessment tools available such as the Disc II as well as many others. If you are going to use assessments it is important to administer it before the final interview for two main reasons. The first is that the assessment should provide some information that you can use to probe further in your final interview. You can compare the information in the assessment to your evaluation of the applicant. The second reason for administering the assessment before the interview is to avoid bias. It's human nature to discredit results from the assessment if you fall in love with the applicant. Therefore, it is better to lead into the interview knowing the applicant's strengths and weaknesses.

I would also like to mention here that you need to ensure that the assessment you select is legally defendable. Make sure it is validated and reliable. This information should be available to you from the seller or test administrator. Also, make sure there is a business reason for administering the test. Some tests can create an adverse impact on hiring minorities and, therefore, can be determined to be discriminatory. You would not administer a math test to manufacturing production workers unless they needed these skills to perform their job. Otherwise, you might find that the test discriminates against certain socioeconomic or protected groups.

THE HIRING DECISION

Now that you have created a well-defined recruiting plan, your decision-making process should be accurate and easier. You have done your preparation work. You have collected a wealth of information in your screening and interview process associated with success factors for the job. You are now ready to select the right candidate and prepare an offer. It is extremely important that you do not let outside emotions and bias impair your decision. Here are a few tips for making good hiring decisions:

- Don't hire overqualified individuals
- Don't hire the first person
- Interview more than one final candidate
- Don't delay your hiring decision because you can lose great candidates if the process is too long
- Don't hire personality over weakness and ability to perform the job
- Don't hire because you are desperate to fill the position
- Do reject candidates after careful examination of your criteria
- Involve your team in the process if you seek additional advice, but make sure the final decision is made by the person who will be managing the candidate
- Evaluate all the information you collected and then sort candidates into buckets (A bucket and B bucket) and note why
- Expect a counter offer and be prepared to negotiate

MAKING THE OFFER

Just because you are making a job offer doesn't mean the candidate will accept. In today's job market, job seekers have many options. Recruiting is like sales, you need to portray and showcase your company to the candidate. There are many reasons why someone will or will not accept your offer. The candidate experience in the hiring process and their willingness to accept the job offer can be affected by the following:

- How well did you treat the candidate during the recruiting process?
- Did you communicate regularly or just leave them hanging?
- Did you treat them as a customer with respect, courtesy, and professionally?
- Did you thank them for their time and interest in your company?

> Recruiting is like sales, you need to portray and showcase your company to the candidate.

Even when conversing with candidates you will not hire, it is important to treat them all in this way. You want everyone to form a positive image of your company if for no other reason other than it is the right thing to do, regardless of the impact they have on your company's reputation through social media outlets.

Hopefully, you have formed a relationship with candidates as they moved through your recruiting funnel. Staying informed and connected during the recruiting process can be crucial so as not to lose your top candidates. For example, find out if they are interviewing with other companies and if so, where are they in this process? Don't be afraid to ask the candidate not to accept another offer without notifying you first.

I typically recommend having a conversation with the candidate before sending the offer letter to discuss some of the details. This is much more effective than an email because you can convey your excitement as well as get a feel for their enthusiasm. Be enthusiastic and don't worry about your enthusiasm affecting the salary negotiation. When deciding upon the pay, use the 10% rule. Generally speaking, someone will look for a 10% pay increase to change jobs. For those who are unemployed, they will typically remain close to their most current pay. Even if a candidate says they are willing to accept a significant pay decrease, carefully consider the likelihood of them leaving your company as soon as a better offer presents itself.

During your call, explain the salary, bonus, benefits, and other perks. Convey to them that you will be sending a formal offer letter. In the offer letter, include the following:

- The salary
- Bonus if applicable
- Benefits and eligibility date
- Position/ job title
- Start date
- Name of supervisor
- Expiration date of the offer
- Statement that offer is contingent on a background check
- Signature line for employee
- Signature line for company representative making the offer

Get a commitment from the candidate, even if it is a tentative one. "What are your thoughts?" "How does this offer sound to you?" Most candidates will want to consider your offer and get back with you. If you detect any hesitation, ask questions about their thoughts about the offer and clarify anything that they might be unsure about. Some candidates might express that they would like to negotiate the salary or something else such as paid time off.

NEGOTIATING THE OFFER

Some of my best hires have come after intense salary negotiation. What is key here is to make sure that the negotiation is a win/win situation leaving both you and the employee feeling valued and appreciated. Know ahead of time the salary range and top limit you are willing to negotiate. You can determine this by considering the fair market salary range for your geographical area as well as looking at your organization and the level of the job and experience needed. You will also need to consider your company culture and any equity issues that could be caused by an increase in the offer. The bottom line here is how serious are you about getting this candidate and what are you willing to pay.

> Some of my best hires have come after intense salary negotiation.

CONCLUSION

In this chapter, we focused on the hiring process—from the job postings through the screening, interviewing, and selection phases. A consistent recruiting process limits your risk for allegations of discrimination and unfair hiring practices. Implementing the Right Source Method and using a recruiting funnel process will improve your selection results but you are not finished here. Retaining these new hires should be your next primary objective and it is the focus of the next two chapters.

CHAPTER SIX
TRAINING AND DEVELOPMENT STRATEGIES

The purpose of this chapter is to address the basics when planning training and development programs for your employees. It is not intended to provide you with a blueprint for developing courses and material, but rather to get you thinking about training and how you will develop and train your employees. First let's consider the business case for training.

WHY TRAINING IS GOOD FOR BUSINESS

Training new employees is an essential part of the onboarding process and it is good for business. In today's economy, many businesses look for ways to cut costs. Often training is a target because it costs money. Can training really add to your bottom line? First ask yourself, does customer retention add to your bottom line? You may be thinking, what does customer retention have to do with training employees? Well, while marketing might get you new customers, great customer service retains existing customers. Many companies spend a significant part of their operating budget on marketing and advertising to grow their business but fail to evaluate and address their customer service delivery. If you haven't evaluated your customer service delivery, you might find that you are losing customers at the same rate you are adding customers.

> Training new employees is an essential part of the onboarding process and it is good for business.

We know that companies that invest in customer service training see improvement in customer retention and employee retention. Their employees can differentiate between excellent customer service and poor customer service and they know how to develop a proactive customer service approach instead of a reactive approach. They are equipped with the tools and techniques needed for handling irate customers and skills to resolve customer complaints. They learn how to identify and deal with workplace stress and conflict.

We also know that a motivated customer service employee will work better and harder. Many organizations realize that these highly motivated employees can really make a difference.

How do you create an environment that motivates and engages employees to be their best?

Establish a motivation partnership between the manager and the employees. Supervisors and managers benefit from training in this area as they learn communication skills and motivation strategies to support their employees. To attain the highest level of customer service delivery, training for the supervisors and managers is as important as the training for the customer service employee.

> Training can help your company create a culture of investing in your people.

In addition to adding to your bottom line, training can help your company create a culture of investing in your people. Employees who have opportunities for growth coupled with supportive managers are more likely to stay. The benefits of training and development apply to both the company and the employees. Here are some of the major benefits:

COMPANY BENEFITS:

- Demonstrate to employees that your company invests in their people
- Improve work efficiency by teaching workforce new skills necessary to do their job
- Initiate better customer service, work safety practices, and improve worker productivity resulting in financial gain
- Increase employee retention
- Improve recruitment success because your company not only says they invest in their people, but they actually do
- Enhance risk management related to employee safety, sexual harassment, and diversity
- Enhance company values by educating employees on ethics, core values, and company mission

EMPLOYEE BENEFITS

- Increase job satisfaction and morale because they see you value them and invest in them
- Increase employee motivation and engagement because they learn new skills
- Increase capacity to adopt new technologies and methods because they acquire new skills and build their confidence in the process
- Increase innovation in strategies and products because they have opportunities to explore, create, and contribute to the company
- Reduce employee turnover because you provide them opportunities to learn new and different tasks that provide opportunities for advancement

HOW TO SET UP A TRAINING PROGRAM IN YOUR COMPANY

Now that you are convinced training is good for business, let's explore how to plan and implement your training program so that these benefits are truly achieved and realized.

You must define the needs of your company. In general, all companies have the overall desire to improve, but have you identified the areas for growth? You may want to include your management team or perhaps create a small committee comprised of managers and key employees to help you with this process. You can collect this information through focus groups, one-on-one meetings with the employees or through a survey.

Take a moment to answer these questions and write your responses to the questions that apply to your company.

This exercise will help you determine your training needs.

- What training can elevate your company to reach expected business outcomes?
    - » How can you empower your employees to accelerate?
    - » How can you improve the effectiveness of your management team?
    - » What are the troubled areas in your company? (such as employee turnover, customer retention, worker inefficiency)
    - » What is keeping you from reaching your business goals?
- What areas do your managers think that their employees need training?
    - » What are the trouble areas in their work group?
    - » What training can improve employee performance?
    - » What training can empower and motivate employees?
- What are your employees saying they need?
    - » What are they interested in learning?
    - » What training would help them succeed in their current role?
    - » What training would help them advance?
- What training already exists in your company and how effective are these initiatives?
- What training is necessary for the future? (new products, services, work procedures)
- Who is the audience? Create a list of positions that your training program should include.

DESIRED BUSINESS OUTCOMES

Now it is time for you to formulate your training plan by identifying your desired business outcomes. In other words, what is your expected business outcome for the training? These outcomes can be specific to an individual employee, group of employees, or the entire company. These outcomes are then stated as training goals and used later to evaluate your training. A training goal can increase revenue, improve organization efficiency, or teach an employee a particular skill. When you launch a new product or service, you will most likely train employees for this as well. Here are examples of business/training goals:

- Increase customer retention
- Increase close rates of sales presentations
- Improve management skills for dealing with employee relations, which contributes to increased employee retention and employee satisfaction
- Increase productivity for newly hired employees
- Reduce errors in work transactions

What are your business outcomes for training? Create a list below:

_____

_____

_____

_____

_____

_____

_____

TYPICAL TOPICS OF EMPLOYEE TRAINING

After answering these questions, you can formulate the topics that address these business outcomes. Each company is different, but in general most companies find there are common themes that surface. Below is a list of typical training topics.

- Technology Skills
- Customer Service
- Sales Training
- Communications
- Diversity
- Ethics and Company Values
- Conflict Resolutions
- Stress Management
- Work Productivity
- Quality Initiatives
- Workplace Safety
- Sexual Harassment
- Legal Compliance
- Management Training
- Leadership Development
- Team Building
- Job Skills
- Company Policies and Procedures

Once you have identified your desired business outcomes and training goals, pair these with the topics for your training and create a training plan. The next table is an example of this process.

Training Topics	Business Outcomes/ Training Goal
Customer Service—Dealing with Difficult Customers	To increase customer retention
Sales Training—Closing the Sale and Overcoming Objections	Increase close rates of sales presentations
Conflict Resolution— Managing Conflict in the Workplace	Improve management skills for dealing with employee relations, which contributes to increased employee retention and employee satisfaction
Job Skills & Company Values—Onboarding New Employees	Increase productivity for newly hired employees and assimilation into the company culture
Job Skills & Work Productivity—Job Shadowing with a Pro	Reduce errors in work transactions and enhance skills for completing work

EXERCISE:

List the business outcomes you identified in the previous exercise and then identify the training topics that relate to these outcomes or training goals.

Training Topics	Business Outcomes/ Training Goal

TYPES OF TRAINING

Once you have identified your training topics and business outcomes, you must then decide on the type of training that is best suited. Training can be delivered in a variety of methods. For example, training can include job shadowing, which is where one employee works alongside another employee and learns how to perform certain job duties. Training can also be conducted in a classroom setting or it can consist of online training where employees complete courses independently.

Below is a list of training options:

On-The-Job Training – This can include job shadowing, reading manuals, reviewing standard operating procedures with a trainer, and internet research.

Technology-Based Training – This includes webinars, interactive videos, online training courses, and other web-based training.

Classroom Training – This can be partial or full-day training presented by internal or external trainers.

Outdoor or Remote Training – This can provide a nice break from the traditional classroom or self-paced online presentations, and often includes team building and goal-setting activities.

Coaching and Mentoring – This gives employees a chance to receive training one-on-one from an experienced professional. Your coaches can be internal employees and managers, or you can hire external coaches.

Planned Reading – This involves reading a book or materials prior to a classroom training or group discussion.

Group Discussions – These are less formal and typically address specific issues or topics.

BUDGET CONSIDERATIONS

The next question you need to ask is "What resources do you have to spend on training?" Even with a small budget for training, you can provide a variety of training and development activities for your employees. You can identify people within your company who can train others or lead discussion groups. You can identify free resources on the internet that provide resources for content.

You will need to collectively gain support and help from others. At one company, we had little money for training and a need to train employees on specific content so they would be prepared to advance to another position. We could not afford to pay for off-site training and we could not afford to hire a trainer or outside consultant. Our solution was to develop the program on our own. First, we located materials to purchase that included a trainer's guide. Next, we solicited employees who were top performers in their field and who could relate to our audience. We asked them to teach one to two chapters or sections in our training manual. These employees were eager to participate as trainers and viewed this as a leadership opportunity. Next, we communicated the benefits of the program and encouraged employees to enroll. We achieved this at a cost of $20 per person. The program was successful because we accomplished our training goals while engaging our employees and investing in their development at a minimal cost.

Depending on the size of your company and the amount of training that needs to occur, you might find it more beneficial to hire a dedicated trainer or to outsource some of the training. You might not have an in-house subject matter expert who can develop and deliver your training. Or you might find that an outside trainer will be perceived in a different way and be more successful in delivering the content. Whomever you select, make sure that not only the content is relevant to your group, but that their presentation and delivery can relate to your group.

DEVELOP A TRAINING PLAN

Now that you have identified your training needs you can create a company training plan. The training plan should include the training topics and format. You must then identify the target audience in need of the training and a completion date or timeline. During this process, it is important to prioritize and decide which training is most important. You can be specific with your dates, or target specific periods as indicated in the example below:

Training Plan		
Training Topic	Target Audience	Date to be completed
Onboarding New Employees	All new employees	First day
Workplace Safety	All employees	First week
Dealing with Difficult Customers	Customer Service Representatives; Sales Associates; Support Admin	First Quarter
Conducting Performance Reviews	Management	Third Quarter
Microsoft Excel— Intermediate and Advanced	Accounting Department	End of Year

Now that you have identified your training topics related to the business outcomes and established your timeline, you simply determine the type of training and execute the plan.

FINAL STEP

The final step in any training program is to evaluate the effectiveness of the training. There are a variety of methods for evaluating training. The primary objective is to measure your business outcomes and track progress in each of the target areas.

One commonly used method is to collect employee feedback such as a course evaluation for each training to determine perceived training effectiveness. Focus on questions pertaining to the application and relevance of the new skills. Consider the employee feedback carefully and adjust your training program accordingly. In order for employees to embrace the training, they must see the value. Course evaluations will indicate the value and perceived benefits from the employee's view point.

Another way to measure training is through objective measurement where managers evaluate employee performance before and after the training. Decide in advance of the training what changes in performance are being observed. Other information can be collected and evaluated, such as customer complaint logs, safety logs, and error incident logs.

You can also measure the effectiveness of your training by observing changes in employee behaviors. Are you noticing a reduction in employee conflict in the work group? Do you observe a shift in the company culture such as increasing cooperativeness and teamwork? What new skills are employees using to make positive changes in their performance?

One final thought is that training should be an everyday occurrence. Encourage your managers and employees to create a culture of learning by finding ways to teach and learn new skills every day. Take the time to demonstrate and explain. Ask employees to reflect on something new they learn each week. Recognize and encourage learning and training accomplishments.

CONCLUSION:

All companies regardless of their size can provide affordable and effective training programs to achieve their business outcomes while developing a culture of investing in your people. Training programs are effective in helping your company achieve their business outcomes, and can be an effective strategy for employee retention, empowerment, and engagement.

CHAPTER SEVEN
EMPLOYEE RETENTION AND ENGAGEMENT STRATEGIES

In this chapter, we will discuss employee retention and employee-engagement, which I believe will have a significant impact on your business's bottom line. We will look at why employee retention is important to company profitability and review factors that impact employee retention and engagement. We will also explore retention drivers that are strategies for retaining employees.

THE COST OF EMPLOYEE TURNOVER

The cost of employee turnover can drain your profit and employee morale. The industry average to replace an employee is 40% of their annual salary. Let's consider you lose five employees who each earn 50,000 per year. The cost of replacing each employee is $20,000. The cost of replacing all five is $100,000. It is important to note that the cost of replacing employees can range from 15% to 150% depending on the position and the significance to the company's operations.

> The cost of employee turnover can drain your profit and employee morale.

Why does turnover cost so much? Turnover cost is more than salary. It includes recruiting cost related to advertising, employee and management cost of those working to fill the position, and many other factors. Here are a few areas that add costs associated with turnover:

Administrative cost	Vacancy cost	Selection and replacement cost
Exit interview	Co-worker overtime	Job advertisement
Administrative functions related to termination (off-boarding)	Added work shifts	Interviewing hours—HR
Separation or severance pay	Temporary workers	Supervisor/ Manager hours
Increase in unemployment rates	Loss of productivity	Background and screening cost
Cobra benefits	Cost of recruiting firm	Training cost

Because turnover is so costly, tracking turnover needs to become part of your monthly reporting along with your profit and loss statement and other financial reporting. When you track and measure something, you place importance and emphasis on it and monitor your progress. You can identify trends and weak areas that need to be addressed. Research shows that high turnover rates predict low performance and companies with lower turnover have a considerable advantage over competitors. It doesn't require much time to gather the data to evaluate your turnover rate and to identify trends. This data is invaluable to you in choosing the necessary changes to address the root causes of turnover.

HOW TO CALCULATE YOUR TURNOVER RATE

All businesses experience employee turnover. When should you be concerned about the level of employee turnover in your company? First you need to determine your turnover rate. The steps for calculating turnover rate are as follows:

1. Calculate the average number of employees during a specific period. Use employee headcount versus FTE (Full Time Equivalent) employees. You can select the number of employees on the 1st, 15th, and 30th of the month and then average them.

2. Calculate the number of separations for that specific period. These include employees who resigned, retired, or were terminated. Do not include those on leave or temporary workers who left.

3. Divide the number of separations by the number of employees and then multiply by 100:

   # of separations/Avg # of Employees x 100

To track annual turnover rate, you simply add the turnover rate (TR) for each month and then average this.

Below is a sample of the turnover calculation for the first quarter of a company.

Turnover Calculation	Number of Employees Separated During Month	Average Number Employees During Month	Turnover Rate (Monthly)
January	3	75	4.00%
February	1	69	1.45%
March	2	73	2.74%
1st Quarter			8.19%

What is your turnover rate? Use the table below to calculate your turnover rate:

Turnover Calculation	Number of Employees Separated During Month	Average Number Employees During Month	Turnover Rate (Monthly)
1st Quarter			
2nd Quarter			
3rd Quarter			
4th Quarter			
Average Annual Turnover			

ANALYZE YOUR RESULTS

Now that you have calculated your turnover rate, you need to determine what it means. Employee turnover is a normal part of the business, and employees may leave for personal circumstances that have nothing to do with how much they enjoy working for you. Turnover can be a good thing, especially when you bring in fresh talent who contribute new ideas and a new sense of energy, or when you lose an employee who earns substantially more due to their longevity and you can bring in less experienced employees at a lower compensation level.

Your goal here is to retain valued employees. How do you determine when turnover becomes excessive? Average turnover rates range from 9%-15% in most studies and can be as high as 60% in some industries such as retail.

You can analyze turnover rate based on any of the following:

- Compare year to year within your company
- Compare month to month within your company
- Compare to your industry
- Compare to your geographic market

How does your turnover rate compare to your industry? You can check the U.S. Bureau of Labor Statistics or industry trade journals to identify average annual turnover rates for your type of business.

UNDERSTAND WHY YOUR EMPLOYEES ARE LEAVING

More important than your turnover rate is the reasons employees are leaving. A high employee turnover rate can affect the bottom line of all businesses.

The negative effect employee turnover has on a small business can be damaging and debilitating.

Employees who are satisfied with their job usually don't quit, so a high turnover rate typically means there is a problem.

I recommend two strategies in particular—exit interviews and stay interviews—that will help you monitor the pulse on employee turnover and determine reasons for employees leaving.

EMPLOYEE EXIT INTERVIEWS

The exit interview can help you diagnose employee turnover and address situations moving forward. It is a strategy for understanding what employees think of your company and your company culture. To obtain honest results, I recommend giving the employee the exit interview questionnaire prior to them leaving. After they complete the questionnaire, I then conduct a meeting to discuss their responses.

Who should conduct the meeting? The interviewer doesn't have to be the direct manager or an HR professional. It is best practice to select someone in your company who is a neutral manager and a good interviewer. Select someone who is a good listener, not overly empathetic, and who will not take offense when the employee vents or becomes emotional.

The exit interview questionnaire provides structure and a guide for your conversation during the meeting. Taking notes during the process as an accurate reflection of the conversation can provide valuable information that is not necessarily obtained on the questionnaire.

There are a variety of topics you can include in your questionnaire related to compensation, benefits, company culture, management issues, training, and opportunities for growth. Below are questions to consider for your exit interview questionnaire.

- How do you feel things went here?
- How did the job match your expectations?
- Do you feel you had the tools and resources to do your job well?
- Do you have suggestions for improvements?
- Do you feel that the work that you were doing aligned with your personal goals and interests?
- Were you comfortable talking to your manager about work issues?
- How would you describe the culture of our company?
- What does your new company/position offer that made you decide to leave our company?
- What could we have done that would have stopped you from leaving?
- Are there any unresolved issues or additional comments?
- How likely are you to recommend a friend to work at our company?
- Would you like us to stay in touch to let you know about future opportunities? Can you also please let us know as you gain new skills and experience?

Be sure to include a comments section after each question to obtain additional information. I typically refrain from sharing the results with others until after the employee has departed from the company. I explain to the employee when they are given the questionnaire and at the start of our meeting that their comments will remain confidential until they leave the company to encourage them to be open and honest with their responses.

Although exit interviews can give a unique perspective on your company's performance related to employee satisfaction, it is not a proactive strategy. Unfortunately, it doesn't prevent the employee from leaving. A proactive strategy is to use employee stay interviews, which enable you to collect information while an employee is still working and can prevent them from leaving.

EMPLOYEE STAY INTERVIEWS

Stay interviews help you understand why employees stay so that important job and company satisfaction factors can be reinforced. I like to compare stay interviews to the 10,000-mile check-up for my car. In order to keep my car running smoothly, I take my car to the auto shop for regular maintenance to have the oil changed, brakes checked, and tires rotated. This regular, proactive maintenance activity keeps the car continuing to run well and enables me to get the car fixed as needed to avoid it breaking down and leaving me stranded.

You need to conduct the same maintenance strategy with your employees through stay interviews.

You can do this by conducting regular informal meetings with your employees. Managers meet with their employees on a consistent basis, such as quarterly, and have check-in meetings where they can engage with their employees. During these meetings, your goal is to find out what the employee likes and dislikes. You will seek information regarding how to support their career growth, whether there is respect in the workplace, and how to energize them. Here is what one of those conversations might look like:

"I'm going to be conducting regular meetings with everyone on my team to see how things are going. This is a time for us to discuss what is going right with your job and what could be better. My role is to help you

succeed by understanding the focus of your work and any challenges you are experiencing."

Here are some other questions you can ask your employees during this meeting:

- What is going well in your job? What will keep you here? What might entice you away?
- What issues or concerns do you have? What would help you succeed in your job? What can I do to help you succeed? What recommendations do you have?
- What is most exciting or energizing about your work? Are we using your talents to the highest potential? If not, what can we do better? What would you really enjoy doing?

Conclude the meeting by thanking them and letting them know you are going to take their recommendations under consideration. Tell them their feedback is important to you and you might share their ideas and recommendations with others (if relevant). Identify your next meeting date and review any actions or recommendations that need to be completed by you or the employee. Document their comments and the actions and recommendations that might need to be addressed before the next meeting. The information in these notes will help you when you conduct your next meeting with the employee.

I recommend that managers conduct these meetings, however some companies opt to conduct employee surveys and focus groups with small groups of employees without the managers participating. The one-on-one approach is more personal and sends a message to employees that you value their feedback and are investing in them.

WHY ARE YOUR EMPLOYEES QUITTING?

Although compensation is always a consideration, if your

compensation is competitive in the market, then other factors affect turnover. Each year research is conducted on the topic of why employees quit their job. This research is conducted annually because of market changes and workplace trends. It is advisable to keep informed of current research reports as trends are identified that enable you to implement changes to address turnover before it becomes an issue to your bottom line. Below is a list of the most common reasons given for employee turnover:

Relationship with their manager. Employees who have managers who support them without micromanaging them are more likely to stay. The manager who provides regular feedback, support, and spends time one-on-one with their employees build successful relationships with employees. Not getting along with your manager is the number one reason employees quit.

Misalignment of employee's skills and the job. This means that the job doesn't match the employee's skills. Either the job is too difficult, and the employee struggles to perform, or the job is not challenging enough, and the employee is bored and goes looking for greener pastures.

Employees are not engaged. Employers need to engage employee's creativity and innovation. Employees seek jobs where they know the company's business goals and feel they are contributing to them.

Management recognition of employee job performance does not occur. Recognizing and rewarding employee's good work is part of developing a strong company culture. Most of us want to know when we are doing a good job and feel appreciated.

Company culture is not supportive. Employees want a company culture comprised of respect, inclusion, fair and competitive compensation, benefits, and rewards. Transparent communication and having managers available and approachable are desired by most employees as well.

Relationships with coworkers are lacking. Having position relationships with coworkers and working constructively as a team are important. Many of us spend as much time (or even more) with our coworkers as we do with our family members. The relationships we have with our coworkers strongly influence our satisfaction at work.

Career-development opportunities are lacking or do not exist. Employees seek a career-development program that provides opportunities for them to learn new skills and see a path for continued growth in the company.

As you gather information about why your employees are quitting their jobs, the next step is to address the primary issues you identify. We have discussed many strategies addressing some of these topics in previous chapters. Let's review the information in the chart below.

Turnover Issue	HR Function	Resolution
Misalignment of skills on the job and mismatch to company culture	Recruiting Strategies	Understanding what makes a good hire. Developing a recruitment strategy to better align jobs with people. Properly assessing candidates for this fit.
Employees leaving for higher paying jobs.	Compensation Strategies	Ensuring you have competitive compensation and benefits to attract and retain employees.

Employees unhappy about company benefit offerings.	Compensation Strategies	Identifying your company perks and communicating these benefits to potential hires and current employees. Provide compensation summaries each year to your employees.
Employees not engaged. Lack of employee recognition by management.	Stay Interviews	Discovering what is important to your employee and how to motivate them. Giving positive feedback regarding their work.
Employees not connecting and supported by management.	Training	Providing management training on topics related to effective management skills—communication, providing feedback, conflict resolution, employee motivation.
Positive relationships with co-workers is missing.	Training	Providing an on-boarding process that includes assimilation with team members. Providing employee training related to working with others, managing conflicts, and respect in the workplace. Plan events for employees to socialize.

WHY ARE YOUR EMPLOYEES LEAVING?

Regardless of whether you have conducted an exit interview with employees who have left your company, you most likely know some of the reasons they are leaving. It can be helpful to keep a list, so you can identify patterns and trends. Here is a sample of how you can gather and track this information:

Employee Name	Termination date	Reason for Leaving	Department

RETENTION DRIVERS

In the next section, we review additional ways to address turnover issues. The purpose is to provide you a general overview of the programs and strategies that will address your turnover issues. These strategies are the retention drivers you can use to keep employees from leaving your company. Employee compensation (wages) and training programs, which we have previously discussed in Chapters Three and Six, can be key elements used when choosing the focus of your retention driver programs.

CAREER-DEVELOPMENT PROGRAMS

Studies indicate that up to 75% of employees want career-development opportunities and a lack of these opportunities fuel early exits. You cannot afford to ignore this statistic. By providing career-development for your employees you gain a competitive advantage and will likely increase your employee retention rates. Invest the time to develop your people.

> Studies indicate that up to 75% of employees want career-development opportunities

There is an important difference between training and career-development. Training focuses on developing and delivering instructional programs to improve employee performance and to learn new skills. Training programs are designed to reach specific business outcomes. Career-development focuses on the employee's personal interests and goals and is individualized for each employee.

Your company's career-development program is a major strategy for empowering, engaging, and retaining employees. In a nutshell, it is a blueprint for the employee to follow that provides opportunities for growth and development. These programs also help you identify future staffing needs and match organizational needs with individual abilities. They provide ongoing learning opportunities to support future growth of both the employee and the company.

What do career-development programs look like? Learning happens all the time on the job. An employee makes a mistake and learns how to correct the mistake or perhaps stumbles across new information related to his job. An employee-development program requires you to intentionally focus on a learning plan for individual employees. Your goal is to establish a learning environment that is informal, safe, and supportive. The learning environment should include input from the employee regarding their interests and work knowledge based on real examples. Employees should be given an opportunity to practice new skills and obtain feedback on how they are doing.

In the previous chapter related to training, we discussed a variety of training methods for delivering training to your workforce. These same methods can be used as development tools for your career-development program. Below is a list of these training methods as well as some new development tools as indicated with an asterisk (*).

- On-the-job training
- Technology-based training
- Classroom training
- Coaching and mentoring
- Planned reading and group discussions
- *Job rotation
- *Job enlargement
- *Job enrichment
- *Increased job responsibilities
- *Developmental assignments

Since we have already discussed some of the training methods listed above, let's review the new methods indicated with an *.

Job Rotation: Job rotation is where employees learn more skills by moving from job to job. It removes the monotony and boredom of doing the same work repeatedly. Job rotation also provides an opportunity for the employee to learn new skills and discover new career opportunities they might never have considered before.

Job Enlargement: Job enlargement is where you expand the employee's current job by adding more tasks and duties. By adding more tasks, you also remove the routine of the job and give the employee the ability to learn something new and stay engaged.

Job Enrichment: Job enrichment is adding depth to the job such as more control, responsibility, and discretion. Here the employee may gain control over the way they complete their work. Management relinquishes some of their power, which allows the employee to be empowered and energized. None of us like being told how and what to do every day.

Increased Job Responsibility: Increased job responsibility involves employees taking on new responsibilities, such as a team lead or a supervisory role. Giving employees added responsibilities is a way to develop and determine your future leaders in the organization.

Developmental Assignments: Developmental assignments allow employees to develop new skills and knowledge related to promotion and advancement opportunities. Not all employees are interested in being or equipped to become managers, but they might be interested in other promotional opportunities in a senior level role within the organization.

THE BLUEPRINT TO YOUR CAREER-DEVELOPMENT PROGRAM

Create a list of questions to ask the supervising manager and the employees. This list can be used as a blueprint for the career-development program. Here are some questions to consider:

- What job competencies in the job description can be further developed?
- What development tools can be used to develop these competencies?
- What new tasks and/or duties would the employee like to learn?
- What opportunities are there to increase the employee's level of responsibility or discretion?
- What controls could they take over?
- What assignments could help them develop new skills or knowledge?
- What is something new the employee would like to learn to do in the company? (this might not be related to their current job)

- As your company grows, what will your workforce need to keep up with this growth?
- What new opportunities will be available to employees as a result of growth or vacancies due to turnover?

EXERCISE

This exercise will help you and your managers craft your employee-development program. Create a list of questions to help guide you through the development of the career-development program. Use the list provided above to create your own blueprint.

Individual Career-Development Plan: Now that you have created your list of questions, meet with your employees and collect information from these discussions so that you can create a customized development plan for each employee. I suggest sending your employees the list of questions before you meet and ask them to come prepared to discuss them. The plan can list some or all of the development activities reviewed in this chapter. Below is a template you can use to list the development opportunities for each employee.

Individual Career-Development Plan	
Employee Name:	
Job Enlargement. List additional work tasks and duties to add. List tasks and duties to remove.	
Job Enrichment. List additional responsibilities and control over specific duties or work. These are duties that the employee gains power over the way in which the work will be accomplished.	

Increased Job Responsibilities. List areas where the employee can take a lead or supervisory role. Leading a committee or initiative at work is an example.	
Developmental Assignments. List work assignments where employees can learn new skills and knowledge that they would need for future promotion.	
Job Rotation. Identify a job in the company where the employee can learn new skills and reduce the monotony of their current position.	
Training Activities. List the training activities (on-line, classroom, and group learning) for the employee to complete.	
Coach/Mentor. Identify someone in the company who will meet with the employee to check progress of the career development and provide feedback. This can be a senior-level peer or manager.	

Once developed, the career-development plan is the responsibility of the employee, not the manager. Employees should participate in crafting their development plan and agree to the activities. They must own it and realize that the company is providing guidance, but ultimately, they must take charge and complete the tasks.

Assign a Coach or Mentor to work with each employee who will regularly check in with the employee to review their progress and provide assistance as needed. Simply creating a career-development plan and reviewing it once a year will typically produce poor results. People perform to what is being measured or mentioned. Plan one-on-one meetings with your employees to review the individual career-development plan at minimum on a quarterly basis. Acknowledge their accomplishments and discuss troublesome areas. This is a great vehicle for managers to recognize employees.

Your company's career-development program is one of the most important weapons you can use to combat the war for talent by offering employees growth and engagement experiences. Hiring employees is only half of the battle. The other half is to retain them and ensure they are up to speed and performing at capacity as soon as possible. Developing an onboarding process after hiring an employee is important. Let's review an onboarding process and a sample of what it looks like in action.

> Your company's career-development program is one of the most important weapons you can use to combat the war for talent.

ONBOARDING

Onboarding is the process through which new employees acquire knowledge, skills, and behaviors to become effective in their new role. Companies that provide new-hire onboarding have higher employee retention rates than those that do not. Onboarding should be part of your company training program and is a useful retention driver. I like to think of it as a mini training plan to kick-start new employees. Proper onboarding will affect the future success of your employees working for your company. Taking the time to plan how new hires will be assimilated into your organization will affect their future performance, their ability to achieve stated goals, and their overall satisfaction with their new positions. Below is an example of the onboarding process.

Before the first day: It is much easier to plan in advance. Before the first day, you should prepare your new-hire paperwork and meet with the managing supervisor to discuss and determine the roles, goals, and projects for the new hire. You want to have the employee's workstation prepared and provide access to your systems. Get your new employee to work immediately. It is also best practice to email the employee prior to the first day with detailed instructions on how to get to the office, where to park, what time to report and who to report to.

On the first day: On the first day, you should introduce your new employee to co-workers and send an introduction email welcoming him/her to the team. You will also want to give your new employee a tour of the office. During the first day, you will want to explain the expectations and go over important work processes. You might also want to schedule a lunch or social activity with the team to help induct the new employee into the company culture.

During the first week: During the first week, you want to assign the first project and go over the expectations and deadlines. This is when you want to discuss long- and short-term goals and the timely manner in which these are to be completed. Defining and demonstrating clear performance expectations are critical to successful onboarding and your employee's future success with your company. At the end of the first week you may want to have an end-of-the-week check-in meeting to discuss any questions or concerns with your new hire.

During the first 30-90 days: During the first month, you need to plan routine check-in meetings and continue building opportunities for employee feedback. The next 30-90 days is the time to invest in training, assign a mentor, and allow for job shadowing. At the end of this period you will want to conduct a 30- or 90-day review and evaluate employee performance and overall job satisfaction.

COMPANY CULTURE

One of the most important factors affecting employee retention and engagement is company culture. Company culture differs from company to company. Whether you are intentionally building your company culture or doing nothing about it, you have a company culture. Your company culture will either contribute to retaining employees or it will be a primary reason employees leave your company. Company culture can support or work against your retention drivers.

Employee-engagement; Relationship with Managers; Relationship with Co-Workers; Compensation; Rewards and Recognition and Training and Development are some of the many factors that reflect your company culture. These factors range from your company size to practices and beliefs that your management team executes and models. They are also a good barometer for how employees interact and their behaviors. Here is a list of what shapes your company culture:

- Company size
- Attitudes
- Environment
- Communication

- Policies
- Common behaviors
- Procedures
- Relationships
- Mission
- Leadership
- Values/Ethics
- Recruiting
- Employee commitment
- Support

When evaluating your company culture examine attributes that give you perspective on how your company culture is viewed by others. Below are a few of these attributes:

- Respect
- Fairness
- Trust
- Integrity
- Teamwork
- Communication
- Collaboration
- Humility
- Accountability
- Adaptability
- Service
- Responsibility
- Engagement
- Honesty
- Growth
- Satisfaction

Ask yourself, what decisions are being made in the organization and how do they align with these attributes? What practices or policies are supporting or NOT supporting your company culture or values?

As your company changes, your company culture may also shift. As start-up companies grow, they experience changes brought about by the increasing company size that present challenges to maintain their company culture. Similar challenges are faced when a company acquires or is acquired by another company and two different company cultures compete against each other. What will the new company culture look like? What are you hoping will remain the same and what is going to change?

We have addressed strategies in previous chapters that will shape your company culture, including recruitment, training, and compensation. In this chapter, we take an in-depth look to evaluate your company culture. Here are a few questions to get you started in this process:

- How do you describe your company culture?
- How do your managers describe your company culture? How do your employees describe your company culture?
- How do outsiders (vendors, previous employees, customers) describe your company culture?
- Do your perceptions of your company culture align with the perception of others?

Collect your information wisely from a variety of sources before you answer this last question. Look back on information collected during exit interviews or conversations with employees. Ask your managers for their input and perhaps ask employees through an employee satisfaction survey. Here are questions to ask to evaluate your company culture:

- How well do employees work together, especially when dealing with conflict?

- Are employees encouraged to speak up and identify problems?
- Does the company address problems head on or allow them to fester?
- Do managers encourage employees to provide new ideas and encourage their development?
- Do managers provide regular feedback to employees, both positive and constructive?
- Would you describe your company management style as one that micromanages or allows for employee autonomy whenever possible?
- What does your company value as a whole?
- Are employees rewarded for their performance? How?
- What are your company's hiring and firing practices? How do they affect your culture?
- Why do employees leave your company?

Once you have collected this information you can better describe your company culture. Think of it as a state of the union report. Create a description that relates to the company culture as it is today, based on the feedback you have collected, not how you would like it to be perceived.

Your answers to these next two questions will aid you in painting an image of your company culture. List your response to these questions in the areas below each.

What practices, policies, and behaviors are shaping your company culture?

_____

_____

_____

_____

Is there anything that you would like to change about your company culture? For example, "I would like to increase employee-engagement by including them in more decision-making opportunities." Or "I would like to increase trust between employees and management." List your comments that describe cultural change.

HOW TO IMPLEMENT CHANGE

What practices, programs or policies can help you implement this change process? For example, do you want your company culture to reflect great customer service both internally and externally? Then you need to instill a culture that provides great service to your customers and also between co-workers and teams. In a company culture based on great service, employees are expected to provide the same level of service to each other that they would to your customer base. Make sure that all new hires have great customer service skills. You may also want to implement training classes that address customer service and perhaps develop guidelines for customer service expectations that you communicate to employees.

Take it a step further by including customer service as a major component on your performance review evaluations. Managers need to recognize employees for great customer service and celebrate success stories. Employees need to recognize their co-workers for their support. You see how these programs work together supporting the culture of exemplary customer service? Who would say no to this type of company culture?

Goal: Establish an exemplary customer service "attitude" where employees are supporting the customers and each other.	
Programs to support this goal:	
Action Items:	

Another example is based on looking beyond the surface in troubled areas to develop a culture of respect in the workplace. This kind of mutual respect is essential to happy employees. Happy employees are better equipped to provide exemplary customer service, which feeds right back into our first example of a winning company culture. In addition to training, rewards and recognition programs based on specific results and behaviors can have a significant effect on your company culture. Awarding an employee for giving great customer service creates a culture that implements and applies your company values.

Managers and team members alike can recognize each other for good deeds. One of my clients created magnetic thank you notes in post card size that were issued to employees so they could recognize team members when they did something special. Another company during their town meetings with employees would recognize employees for their accomplishments and performance. I created a large bulletin board in the main work area that displayed customer notes complimenting different employees.

Take a moment to complete the following for your company culture initiatives:

Goal:	
Programs to support this goal:	
Action Items:	
Who can help you?	

MANAGEMENT PRACTICE

Employee-engagement is viewed as one of the most significant single factors in determining future success of your company. The managers of your company, including you, either support employee-engagement or suffocate it. Therefore management practice is also a major retention driver because engaged employees typically enjoy their jobs and tend to remain working for you.

No matter which employee motivation theory you accept, all of them reference factors about relationships between managers and their employees. The phrase, *It starts at the top* depicts the importance of management in shaping company culture. These relationships highly contribute to your company culture in either a positive or negative way. No matter what type of employee programs you establish or how well you compensate your employees, ineffective managers damage your company culture and cause employees to leave their jobs. It is as important to evaluate and address your management practices as it is your overall company culture.

Below are questions to help you evaluate your managers and how they contribute to the development of your company culture. As you answer these questions, you will assess each manager's effectiveness.

- How effective are your managers in leading their employees? Are they able to persuade them and build team camaraderie?
- Do they encourage employees to be creative and innovative by supporting their ideas?
- How do they make decisions? (unilaterally or include their subordinates)
- How do they manage conflict? (head on, avoid it until it festers, or dominate the situation)
- How often do they provide feedback to their employees? What type of feedback do they provide? (both positive and negative or only negative)
- Are they a micromanager or do they give employees latitude regarding how they complete their work? Do they give the employee too much control?
- How do they communicate with their subordinates? (a downward approach or two-way including employees)
- How approachable are they?
- Have they established an open-door policy to minimize conflicts?
- Do their subordinates seem loyal to them?

- What is the employee turnover rate in their department compared to the other areas of the company? Why are their employees resigning?
- How would you describe their overall management style? (Democratic, Persuasive, Authoritarian, Permissive, Consultative, Mentor)

After answering these questions, you can identify aspects of your company culture that each manager supports and areas where they are lacking. Your next plan of action is to identify how you are going to address problematic areas with each manager. You (or someone at the highest levels in the organization) need to take responsibility for developing managers. If you don't start at the top, all of your other employee-engagement and retention programs will be fruitless.

Let's develop a plan of action for addressing these issues. Below is a list of suggested leadership-development activities that builds management skills.

Meet with each manager to conduct a two-way conversation regarding the management questions listed above. Identify problematic areas and discuss how these contribute to the company culture. Include your assessment of their contribution. Ask for their feedback.

Identify training opportunities together that will address problematic areas, such as communication, conflict resolution, and providing feedback

Provide new assignments that will challenge managers to apply new skills they learn in their training.

Locate a mentor or coach that will help them learn new skills and resolve issues. You might want to hire a coach to work with particular managers.

Conduct regular check-in meetings with the manager to discuss their progress. Allow for time to discuss challenges and problem solve together.

Implement action-learning opportunities in your management meetings. Action learning involves building skills while discussing and resolving current business issues. It gives managers the opportunity to apply insights immediately in a structured and supportive way. An example would be discussing employee attendance issues and how to resolve them.

Send them to management training courses or bring in a trainer to conduct training for your managers.

CONCLUSION

Managing employee turnover and retention is important. The cost of not paying attention to these areas affects your bottom line. The problems that arise from this can be exhausting and overwhelming. Let's summarize the strategies for employee retention and the retention drivers to reduce employee turnover:

1. Calculate and analyze your employee turnover
2. Understand why employees are leaving
3. Be proactive by conducting stay interviews
4. Implement effective recruiting strategies to better align jobs with people and properly assess candidates
5. Ensure you have competitive compensation and benefit offers to attract and retain employees
6. Communicate the value of these benefits to your employees by providing a benefit summary to each one
7. Provide management and employee training related to your company core values, respect for others and effective teamwork

8. Invest in your employees by developing and implementing career-development programs for them

9. Provide an onboarding process for all new hires to indoctrinate them to assimilate them into your organization for future success

10. Evaluate your company culture and identify why areas need to be improved

11. Implement programs and action items to support these changes

12. Evaluate your management practices and determine how they support or conflict with your company values and culture

13. Evaluate each manager related to their management practices and effectiveness of engaging, relating, and supporting the employees

14. Develop a plan of action for developing your managers to learn new skills and resolve problematic areas.

This is a comprehensive list and it can seem overwhelming. Take it a step at a time going from the first item on the list to work your way down to the bottom in whatever order works best for you. Seek assistance from your support staff and key managers to help you identify and prioritize which strategies you, and they, can tackle first. Take small steps and regularly focus on this action list, and you will soon recognize your accomplishments.

CHAPTER EIGHT
MANAGING RISK STRATEGIES

This chapter is relatively short compared to the other chapters mainly because when you implement the strategies discussed in the previous chapters, your risk will be greatly minimized. My intention in writing this book was never to focus on the legal aspects of managing people, rather on the strategies related to best practices that produce better results.

When people feel that they are being treated fairly and you have established sound practices for managing the people side of your business, then you reduce your risk.

However, discussing risk is essential to establishing and maintaining effective strategies for managing your human capital and cannot be ignored.

Risk is the main cause of uncertainty in any business. Therefore, the task of identifying risk and managing it before any adverse effect impacts your business is extremely important.

Businesses face many types of risk related to revenue, expenses, quality, scheduling, and their employees. There are types of risk unique to each business and organization model. Below are common risk factors that many companies consider:

- Competitors entering the market
- Economic pressures
- Customer satisfaction and retention
- Increased operating expenses
- Providing quality service or product
- Late customer payments
- Cash flow
- Shortage of labor
- High employee turnover
- Employee theft and fraud

This chapter will focus on risk associated with the people side of the business and address risk management and strategies for best practices.

What is risk management related to your human capital? Even small businesses do not escape the impact of people. If you only employ one person, you will undoubtedly face some type of risk associated with this employee. Your people are a source of risk and your people must know how to handle risk. Knowing what your risks are and staying in front of them is essential for minimizing the financial impact it will have on your company and the disruption it will cause. Consider what risks your company may incur related to losses due to the following:

- The shortage or loss of key employees
- Deterioration of employee morale
- Inadequate development of your employees
- Lack of HR infrastructure to support your operations
- Insufficient work schedules
- Unsafe work environment
- Inequality or inequity in HR management
- Discriminatory conduct
- Ethics and behavior
- Compliance and workforce regulations

THE GOAL OF RISK MANAGEMENT

The goal of risk management is to identify, evaluate, and resolve risk items before they become threats to your organization. When developing a risk management plan for your human resource activities, there are both short-term projects and long-term areas that are important. Risk management should be a primary component of your quality assurance process that minimizes financial risk due to sub-standard work performance, overtime cost associated to poor scheduling, exposure to workplace litigation, benefit regulations, and administrative errors. This general list will get you started but it is important that your company identifies and evaluates risk unique to your company. Some of these risk areas will be relevant and others will be less important.

HR Activity & Potential Risk	Y/N	Potential Considerations
General HR Practices • Discriminatory practices • Privacy breach • Department of Labor fines		Do all company policies and procedures comply with federal and state laws related to leave, equal employment opportunity, sexual harassment, and worker safety?
		Are HR and management practices consistently and fairly applied?
		Are employment records and sensitive information retained in secured areas and only available to those who need access?
		Are employment records retained for the appropriate length of time after an employee is terminated?
		Are state and federal required workplace posters displayed?

Hiring • Discriminatory practices • At-will status • Negligent hiring • ADA compliance • Department of Labor infractions • State workforce infractions • IRS infractions • Workplace litigation		Do you conduct a full screening on all potential candidates?
		Are your interview questions appropriate and legally defendable? (ADA Compliant and non-discriminatory)
		Is your employment application legally compliant?
		Were promises made in the offer letter that cannot be upheld?
		Are you following your city, state, and federal requirements for conducting background checks?
		Did you obtain written authorization to conduct background checks according to the Fair Credit Reporting Act?
		Are your policies and procedures regarding drug testing and the use of arrest and conviction records and other background information compliant with city, state, and federal requirements?
		Does your offer letter include *at-will* language?
		Are you completing all I-9 forms correctly?
		Are you satisfying new-hire reporting (W-4) and state filings?

QUANTIFY THE RISK

After reviewing this list, your next task is to determine the likelihood of an identified threat being released and what its impact could be on your business. Consider what manager's and employee's opinions and perspectives would be regarding these threats. What seems reasonable and what seems improbable? What is the probability that the risk is occurring and what are the costs associated with this risk? You might want to define the risk in three areas:

Major Risk. Large financial loss, operation breakdown or shut down, loss of reputation.

Moderate Risk. Monetary loss from legal action or loss of productivity, adverse impact on workforce, safety, and health, and additional expenses resulting from these situations.

Minor Risk. Relatively low impact (or none) on financial or operations functions, most likely simply not implemented as a best practice.

After defining the level of risk for each, adopt cost-effective methods to resolve each to mitigate your risk. Assign specific actions to employees and managers. Communicate to them that they will be accountable for managing this risk and taking the necessary actions to manage the risk ongoing.

You might want to develop standard operating procedures to ensure and define the process and actions. Standard operating procedures will clarify your processes and be a resource for future hires to use when taking on these responsibilities.

Once the risk analysis is conducted and your action items are identified, it is important to continue to monitor the risk to ensure your solutions are being properly implemented. Incorporate time in your management meeting to review risk areas and ask managers to report on them. At least once a year conduct a risk assessment to ensure there are no new risks developing.

Below is a form that you can use to develop and monitor your action plan:

Risk Area	Corrective Actions	Person Responsible	Due Date	Date Complete
Need to display employ-ment law posters	Order and post law posters	Facility Manager		
Managers not trained on legal employ-ment practices	Provide 2-4 hours of training	Office Manager - hire trainer		
New-hire onboarding	Develop and imple-ment new hire on-boarding process	Office Manager - may need to consult with HR Consultant		

CONCLUSION

Managing risk can be time consuming and daunting, but not managing it can be disastrous. If you doubt this, visit the Equal Employment Opportunity Commission or the Department of Labor and research recent lawsuits for enough information to motivate you to take action. Identify risk areas that need to be corrected for your company. This becomes an important part of your defense once you identify the problem and take immediate action to correct it. Seek a consultant or expert in troubled areas where you need assistance to help you effectively evaluate and create a corrective plan of action. Awareness is critical to managing your risk, so take the time to review your company risk.

CONCLUSION

Managing people is viewed by business owners, CEOs, and managers as one of the most challenging aspects of business. Many of us are subject matter experts in our core business function, but most managers are not experienced or equipped to deal with the diverse challenges of attracting, selecting, and retaining top talent. We each bring our strengths and weaknesses into our businesses and enhance our experience and knowledge to choose the actions and strategies needed to achieve maximum results. Managing human capital can be overwhelming, but it is not impossible.

Taking the time to create a plan for managing the people processes in your business is just as important as creating your sales and marketing plan. Without a clear direction, you might find yourself falling short of achieving your business growth goals.

Begin with the basics by answering these two questions as presented in Chapter 1:

1. What kind of people do I need to manage and run my business in a way that aligns with my business goals?

_____

_____

2. What programs and initiatives should I implement that will attract top talent, achieve employee retention and develop my employees?

_____

_____

At this point, you might be asking yourself, "Where do I begin?"

You have already begun. This book has presented success strategies for the five primary and essential areas I have found necessary in managing human capital. They are:

1. Recruiting Strategies
2. Compensation Strategies
3. Training and Development Strategies
4. Retaining Top Talent Strategies
5. Managing Risk

You might also be asking yourself, "Which initiatives and programs are the best for me?" I recommend you find the pain first—the things that disrupt, obstruct, or cause you the most worry. What could cause you not to reach your business goals? Is it hiring top talent or having an untrained workforce that produces substandard services or products? Is it losing top talent to employers who offer better pay or career-development programs? Or are you dissatisfied with your company culture?

Once you have identified your pain points, review the chapters that relate to your specific concerns. Prioritize your pain points based on the level of importance and fix them by selecting the practices presented in these chapters. The exercises have provided you an opportunity to draft your plan of action.

I recommend that you choose one of the strategies that is most important to your business to work on at a time. For example, if you will be hiring key employees this year, you should focus on the recruiting and hiring chapters. If improving employee retention is an area of concern, begin with Employee Retention and Engagement Strategies.

As you develop and implement human capital strategies, continue to modify and expand your plan and implementation of strategies. Engage key employees and managers to help you and provide feedback. Lastly, know when to ask for help. If you get stuck or something is not working like you expect, engage an outside consultant for the areas or projects where you need help.

FINAL EXERCISE

Developing and implementing human resource strategies is just as important to your business planning as financial and sales planning. However, it does require thought, time, and allocation of resources to grow and maintain your business. This final exercise will enable you to begin this planning process.

1. List the strategies that are most important to you and select the strategy that you want to implement first:

_____

_____

_____

_____

2. Identify team members and managers who you would like to include in the development and implementation of these strategies:

_____

_____

_____

_____

Now that you have these questions answered, you are ready to develop your human resource strategies. You should be excited and enthusiastic, because these strategies will elevate your company and you will begin to see positive results almost immediately. Share your enthusiasm with your key managers and team members. Then sit back and enjoy the fruits of your labor for it doesn't take long to see results from your new endeavors.

Access Documents Online

To access downloadable forms and documents related to the exercises presented in this publication, visit my company website: www.premierhrsolutions.net

RESOURCES

The following list consists of resources that provide regulation information, instructions, and forms.

1. Premier HR Solutions:
    www.premierhrsolutions.net
    To access downloadable forms and documents related to the exercises presented in this publication, visit my company website.

2. Department of Labor:
    www.dol.gov
    To access information related to:
    a. Bureau of Labor Statistics
    b. Occupational Safety & Health Administration (OSHA)
    c. Wage and Hour Division
    d. Equal Employment Opportunity (EEOC)
    e. Family and Medical Leave Act (FMLA)
    f. Employee Retirement Income Security Act (ERISA), (ACA), (COBRA),(HIPAA)
    g. Uniformed Services Employment and Reemployment Rights Act (USERRA)

3. National Labor Exchange:

    www.usnlx.com

    Contains a list of State Workforce Agencies such as:

    a. Texas Workforce Commission
    b. State of California Labor and Workforce
        Development Center

4. U.S. Small Business Administration:

    www.sba.gov

    Contains resources for small employers such as:

    a. Hire and manage employees
    b. Stay legally compliant

5. Internal Revenue Service

    www.irs.gov

    Contains forms and filing information for payroll and payroll
    taxes including W3, W4, W9, and 941.

6. Society for Human Resource Management (SHRM):

    www.shrm.org

    The world's largest professional human resources membership
    association. Membership includes access to news, resources, tools
    and information related to all areas of HR disciplines.

INDEX

A
administrative assistant applicant screening, 55
administrators, HR professionals as, 10
applicant tracking software, 71–72
attendance, 62

B
Baby Boomers, 37
behavioral interview questions, 57–58, 60, 72
benefits, 35–36, 46–47
business outcomes, defining, 86
business strategies, and Human Resources, 11

C
candidates
    needs of, 50
    profiles, 56–57
career-development programs, 28–29, 107–113
career fairs, 27
change, implementing, 119–120
classroom training, 90
coaching, 90, 112–113
company culture, 2, 6, 13, 21–23, 25, 29, 51, 63, 93, 104, 115–119
company values, 14
company website
    career page on, 28

See also social media

compassion, examples of, 4

compensation strategies, 13–14, 16, 31–32, *38*

    communicating, 37, 39

    exercises, 39–47

    non-monetary compensation, 35–36

    and perks/benefits, 33–34

    planning, 33–37

complacency, 22

culture of respect, 14

customer retention, 82

customer service, 119

    importance of, 82

customer-service related questions, 60

D

developmental assignments, 110, 112

discrimination, 13, 52–53, 75, 79

E

employee-engagement, 104, 121–122

    See also company culture

employee referral programs, 26

employee retention, 61, 82–83

    career-development, 107–108, 113

    and compensation packages, 32

employee training, 81–84, 87, 90–91

    See also onboarding training programs; training programs

employees

    as assets, 9

    attitudes of, 12–13

    and boredom, 61–62, 104

    and career-development, 105

    questions about, 85

    quitting, 103–105

employment history, author's, 5–6

examples

administrative assistant applications, 55
candidate profiles, 57
executive assistant requirements, 71
parents', 4–5
exercises, 137–138
career-development programs, 111–113
company culture, 22–23, 117–119, 121
compensation strategies, 39–47
customer service, 120
describe your company, 22–23
jobs/traits, 59–60
recruiting pitches, 24–25
risk management, 130–131, 133
training programs, 85–86, 89
traits, 63–64
turnover rate, 97–98
war on talent, 29–30
workforce planning, 53–54
See also questions
exit interviews, 51, 100–102

F
Fair Labor Standards Act (FLSA), 37
financial outcomes, and employee behaviors, 12–13
first level assessments, 73
Five Strategies, overview, 13–15
5 Tips for Crafting More Effective Job Postings (Gray), 67
funnel approach to hiring, 65, 69, 70, 71, 77, 79

G
Generation X, 37
Gray, Nolan, *5 Tips for Crafting More Effective Job Postings*, 67
group discussions, 90

H

hiring managers, thought processes of, 49–50
hiring. *See* recruitment
Houston, Texas, 1
HR departments, rigidity of, 10–11
HR professionals, as administrators, 10
human capital strategies, 135–137
    questions about, 11–12, 15–17

I

ideal candidates, determining, 52, 56–57
increased job responsibility, 110, 112
individual career-development plans, 111–113
information collection, and trend indication, 51–52, 107
interviewing, 58, 75
    exit interviews, 100–101
    pre-employment assessments, 75
    questions, 61
    stay interviews, 100, 102–103
    template for, *74*

J

job boards, 67–69
job candidates
    making an offer to, 76–79
    treatment of, 27–28, 77
job enlargement, 109, 111
job enrichment, 109, 111
job grouping/ranking, 40–42
job histories, reviewing, 62
job postings, 66–67, 69
job requirements, listing, 59, 71
job rotation, 109, 112
job shadowing, 89, 89–90

L

lagging the market, 33–34
leadership development, 123–124
leading the market, 33–34
Lilly Ledbetter Fair Pay Act, 37

M

managers, 122–123
    relationships with employees, 104, 121–122
mentoring, 90, 112, 113
Millennials, 36–37
motivation, 14, 82–83

N

negative outcomes, of hiring the wrong person, 20
non-monetary compensation, 35–36, 46–47

O

offer letters, 78
on-the-job training, 89–90
onboarding training programs, 29, 81–82, *92*, 113–115
outdoor training, 90

P

passive job seekers, 22
pay grades, determining, 43–46
people management plans, 11
personality types, 57
phone screening, 72
pipelines, for job candidates, 27, 71, *72*
planned reading, 90
pre-employment assessments, 75
primary schools, 2
proactivity, advantages of, 13

Q

questions, 136–137
    about salaries, 72
    about training programs, 85
    to ask job candidates, 50, 57–58, 61
    to ask managers, 110–111
    behavioral interview, 57–58, 60–61
    for candidate profiles, 56
    on company culture, 117–118
    customer-service related, 60
    for exit interviews, 101
    and human capital strategies, 11–12, 15–17, 136
    interview, 61, *74*
    knock-out, 72–73
    on management, 122–123
    on retaining talent, 14
    risk management, 130–131
    for stay interviews, 103
    for your employees, 24–25
    See also exercises

R

reactivity, 22
recruitment, 51, 83
    choosing ideal candidates, 52, 56–57
    making an offer, 76–79
    pitches for, 24–26
    and revenue growth, 20–21
    statistics, 20
    See also interviewing
recruitment processes
    bad examples of, 27–28
    compared to sales, 50, 76–77
    legality of, 52–53, 75
    traits exercise, 63–64
recruitment strategies, 13, 15–16, 19–20
    overlooking, 19

and work experience, 56
relationships, importance of, 2
remote training, 90
research, in the 1980's, 2
resume screening, 72
revenue growth, and recruitment, 20–21
Right Source Method, 21, 49, 54–55, 79
risk management, 15, 17, 83, 128–129
    exercises, 130–131, 133
risks, 128–129, 132

S
salaries, negotiating, 78–79
salary ranges
    information needed to determine, 34–35
    researching, 43
salary requirements, 72
school programs, 3
social media, 68
    taking advantage of, 26–27
    See also company website
standard operating procedures, 132
start-up companies, 36
statistics
    on employee turnover, 29, 95–96
    on recruitment, 19
stay interviews, 100, 102–103
success, determining, 62

T
talent retention, 14, 17
talent wars, 21–22, 26–30, 113
technology based training, 90
Texas, Houston, 1
Texas Association of School Boards, 3
training activities, 112
training and development strategies, 14, 16–17, 90–91

training programs, 14, 83–85, 87, *88*, 89–93, 108
　See also employee training; onboarding training programs
transparency, and compensation strategies, 39
trends
　and information collection, 51–52, 107
　tracking, 68
trust, importance of, 2
turnover rates, 29, 34, 53–54, 84, 95–97, 99, 105–106, 124–125
　calculating, 97–98
　and HR costs, 12–13

W
work experience, 56
workforce planning, 53–54

ABOUT THE AUTHOR

Scholley Bubenik is the principal owner of Premier HR Solutions, a consulting firm dedicated to providing executive-level human resource management to small, medium and start-up companies. Her vision has enabled hundreds of entrepreneurs, business owners, and managers to successfully grow and manage their companies.

Scholley's entrepreneurial roots run deep. In fact, they are literally part of her DNA. From her youngest days she had people in her life who she loved and admired for their willingness to step out and do something different and build something of their own that they could be proud of.

Her grandfather and uncles emigrated to the U.S. in the early twentieth century to avoid religious persecution and found America to be a land of great opportunity. They opened and ran several small businesses. Scholley's mother opened and ran a dress store for years in her hometown of Taylor, Texas.

So, it's no surprise that she, too, started a business in her early twenties after graduating college with her first degree. Her first business was a private primary school. She eventually grew the school to a staff of 25 and it thrived. She admits today that she knew very little at the time about hiring and managing people, but she learned a great deal and succeeded anyway.

Once she met her goals of achieving profitability and national accreditation, Scholley returned to her hometown of Taylor, Texas. When the Taylor school district received a federally funded grant in 1992 to aid childhood literacy in the town, Scholley was chosen to run it. She spent the next seven years teaching parents how to read, and teaching them how to help their kids learn how to read. The initiative was a resounding success and it was chosen by the NEA as one of 12 acclaimed programs across the country.

When that work was over, Scholley began a 20 year career in Human Resource Management, working at the highest level with growing companies and entrepreneurs. During this time, she honed her skills in human resource management before launching Premier HR Solutions, a company that serves other growing companies and advises them on all aspects of human capital. Scholley has helped a wide range of companies across multiple industries establish human resource departments, eventually expanding to work with companies involved in mergers and acquisitions as well as those who required assistance with recruiting services and customized training.

Scholley lives in Lago Vista, Texas with her husband, Rick, They have two daughters, Kristen and Stacy.

CPSIA information can be obtained
at www.ICGtesting.com
Printed in the USA
FSHW020641140419

9 781732 282209